SAY IT
IN CHINESE

SINOLINGUA
BEIJING

First Edition   1981
Second Edition   1996
Second Printing 1999

ISBN 7-80052-048-X

Copyright 1996 by Sinolingua

Published by Sinolingua

24 Baiwanzhuang Road, Beijing 100037, China

Tel: 86-010-68326333

86-010-68994599

Fax: 86-010-68326642

E-mail: sinolingua@ihw.com.cn

Printed by Beijing Foreign Languages Printing House

Distributed by China International

Book Trading Corporation

35 Chegongzhuang Xilu, P.O. Box 399

Beijing 100044, China

Printed in the People's Republic of China

KEY TO PRONUNCIATION

Beginning Consonants

b	b as in *be*
c	ts as in *tsar*, strongly aspirated
d	d as in *do*
f	f as in *food*
g	g as in *go*
h	h as in *her*
j	j as in *jeep*
k	k as in *kind*
l	l as in *land*
m	m as in *man*
n	n as in *nine*
p	p as in *par*
q	ch as in *cheek*
r	r like the *z* in *azure*
s	s as in *sister*
t	t as in *ten*
w	w as in *way*

x	sh as in *she*
y	y as in *yet*
z	ds as in *deeds*
zh	j as in *jump*
ch	ch as in *church*
sh	sh as in *shore*

Vowels and Diphthongs

a	a as in *father*
ai	i as in *kite*
ao	ow as in *how*
an	ahn
ang	like in *song*
e	er as in *her* (Brit.)
ei	ay as in *way*
en	weak form of an as in *and*
eng	no English equivalent but nearly as in *lung*
i	ea as in *eat*
ia	*yah*
ie	ye as in *yes*
iao	yow as in *yowl*
iou	*yee-oh*

ian	ien as in *lenient*
in	een as in *keen*
iang	i-ahng
ing	ing as in *sing*
iong	y-oong
o	aw as in *law*
ou	ow as in *low*
ong	oo-ng
u	oo as in *too*
ua	wah
uo	wa as in *water*
uai	wi as in *wife*
uei	as *way*
uan	oo-ahn
uen	won as in *wonder*
uang	oo-ahng
ueng	like won as in wont
ü*	as "yü" in German
üe	no English equivalent
üan	no English equivalent
ün	no English equivalent

---

* "ü" is spelt so only when it follows "l" and "n", while it is spelt as "u" in all other places.

CONTENTS
目录
Mùlù

1. GREETINGS AND GENERAL CONVERSATION
问候 和 一般 会话
Wènhòu hé Yìbān Huìhuà

Hello! How do you do ?

您 好!

Nín hǎo?

How are you?

您 好 吗?

Nín hǎo ma?

Fine, thanks.

很 好,谢谢。

Hěn hǎo, Xièxie.

Good (morning) (afternoon) (evening)!

(您早)　　(您好)　　　　(晚上好!)

(Nín zǎo) (No equivalent; use Nín hǎo) (Wǎnshang hǎo)!

Good night!

晚安!

Wǎn'ān!

Goodbye!

再见!

Zàijiàn!

We had a (good) (tiring) journey.

我们 的 旅行 很 (顺利)(辛苦)。

Wǒmen de lǔxíng hěn (shùnlì)(xīnkǔ).

What's our programme?

您 给 我们 安排了 什么 活动?

Nín gěi wǒmen ānpáile shénme huódòng?

What's our travel schedule?

我们 的 旅行 计划 是 什么?

Wǒmen de lǔxíng jìhuà shì shénme?

Thanks for meeting us. It was kind of you.

谢谢 您 来 迎接 我们。

Xièxie nín lái yíngjiē wǒmen.

He (She) (They) asked me to give you (you—pl.)
best regards.

他 (她) (他们) 让 我 向 您(你们) 问好。

Tā(tā)(tāmen) ràngwǒ xiàng nín(nǐmen) wènhǎo.

Please give ... my best regards.

请向 ……问好。

Qǐng xiàng...wènhǎo.

Congratulations!

祝贺 您 （你们）!

Zhùhè nín（nǐmen）!

I'm delighted to (know) (see) you.

我 很 高兴 （认识） （见到） 您。

Wǒ hěn gāoxìng（rènshi）（jiàndào）nín.

My name is … This is my (husband) (wife)
(daughter) (son).

我叫 … 这是 我的（丈夫） （夫人）（女儿）

Wǒjiào…Zhèshì wǒde（zhàngfu）（fūren）（nǚér）

（儿子）。

（érzi）.

I'm from Austria. I'm an Austrian.

我 从 奥地利 来。我是 奥地利 人。

Wǒ cóng Āodìlì lái. Wǒshì Āodìlì rén.

Algeria	Argentina
阿尔及利亚	阿根廷
Āěrjílìyà	**Āgēntíng**
Australia	Bangladesh
澳大利亚	孟加拉
Āodàlìyà	**Mèngjiālā**
Belgium	Brazil
比利时	巴西
Bǐlìshí	**Bāxi**

Britain	Myanmar
英国	缅甸
Yīngguó	**Miǎndiàn**
Canada	Denmark
加拿大	丹麦
Jiānádà	**Dānmài**
Egypt	Finland
埃及	芬兰
Āijí	**Fēnlán**
France	Greece
法国	希腊
Fǎguó	**Xīlà**
Guinea	Holland
几内亚	荷兰
Jǐnèiyà	**Hélán**
Iceland	India
冰岛	印度
Bīngdǎo	**Yìndù**
Iran	Iraq
伊朗	伊拉克
Yīlǎng	**Yīlākè**
Italy	Japan
意大利	日本
Yìdàlì	**Rìběn**

4

Jordan	Cambodia
约旦	柬埔寨
Yuēdàn	**Jiǎnpǔzhài**
Korea	Kuwait
朝鲜	科威特
Cháoxiǎn	**Kēwēitè**
Lebanon	Liberia
黎巴嫩	利比里亚
Líbānèn	**Lìbǐlǐyà**
Libya	Malaysia
利比亚	马来西亚
Lìbǐyà	**Mǎláixiyà**
Mali	Mauritania
马里	毛里塔尼亚
Mǎlǐ	**Máolǐtǎníyà**
Mexico	Morocco
墨西哥	摩洛哥
Mòxīgē	**Móluògē**
Nepal	New Zealand
尼泊尔	新西兰
Níbóěr	**Xīnxīlán**
Norway	Pakistan
挪威	巴基斯坦
Nuówēi	**Bājīsītǎn**

Peru
秘鲁
Bìlǔ

Poland
波兰
Bōlán

Romania
罗马尼亚
Luómǎníyà

Somalia
索马里
Suǒmǎlǐ

Sri Lanka
斯里兰卡
Sīlǐlánkǎ

Sweden
瑞典
Ruìdiǎn

Syria
叙利亚
Xùlìyà

Thailand
泰国
Tàiguó

Philippines, the
菲律宾
Fēilùbīn

Portugal
葡萄牙
Pútáoyá

Singapore
新加坡
Xīnjiāpō

Spain
西班牙
Xībānyá

Sudan, the
苏丹
Sūdān

Switzerland
瑞士
Ruìshì

Tanzania
坦桑尼亚
Tǎnsāngníyà

United States, the
美国
Měiguó

Venezuela

委内瑞拉

Wěinèiruìlā

Yugoslavia

南斯拉夫

Nánsīlāfū

Zambia

赞比亚

Zànbǐyà

Yemen

也门

Yěmén

Zaire

扎伊尔

Zhāyīěr

I'm on a people's friendship group tour. I'm (head) (a member) of the group.

我 是 人民 友好 参观团 的 成员。

Wǒ shì rénmín yǒuhǎo cānguāntuán de chéngyuán.

我 是 (团长) (团员)。

Wǒ shì (tuánzhǎng) (tuányuán).

We're (I'm) visiting China on the invitation of (the Academy of Sciences) (the Chinese People's Friendship Association) (the Chinese Medical Association) (the Chinese People's Institute of Foreign Affairs) (the Ministry of Culture) (the Ministry of Foreign Affairs) (the Ministry of Foreign Economic Relations and Trade) (the Women's Federation) (the Trade Union) (the Youth League).

我们　（我）　是　应　（科学院）（中国
Wǒmen（wǒ）shì yìng（Kēxué Yuàn）（Zhōngguó
人民　对　外　友好　协会）（中华
Rénmín Duì wài Yǒuhǎo xiéhuì）（Zhōnghuá
医 学 会）（中国　　人民　　外交　学会）
Yixuéhuì）（Zhōngguó Rénmín Wàijiāo xuéhuì）
（文化　部）（外交　部）（对外　经济
（Wénhuà Bù）（Wàijiāo Bù）（Duìwài Jīngjì
贸易　部）（妇女　联合会）　（工会）
Màoyì Bù）（Fùnǚ Liánhéhuì）（Gōnghuì）
（青　年　团）　的　邀请　而　来　的。
（Qīngniántuán）de yāoqǐng ér lái de.

I've come to China in accordance with our cultural
agreement（to give lectures）（to do research）（to
study）.

我是　根据　文化　协定　来　中国　（讲
Wǒshì gēnjù wénhuà xiédìng lái Zhōngguó（jiǎng-
学）（进行　研究）（学习）的。
xué）（jìnxíng yánjiū）（xuéxí）de.

I've come to see how the Chinese People live.

我　是来　看一看　中国　人民　的　生活
Wǒ shìlái kànyíkàn Zhōngguó rénmín de shēnghuó
情　况　的。
qíngkuàng de.

8

I'm a (teacher) (architect) (artist) (businessman)
(chemist) (dairy farmer, poultry farmer) (doctor) (engineer) (farmer) (lawyer) (physicist)
(trade unionist) (worker) (journalist).

我 是 （教师） （建筑师） （艺术家） （商人）

Wǒshì (jiàoshī)(jiànzhùshī)(yìshùjiā)(shāngrén)

（化学家） （牛奶 场 工人， 家禽场

(huàxuéjiā)(niúnǎichǎng gōngrén, jiāqínchǎng

工人） （医生） （工程师） （农民）

gōngrén) (yīshēng) (gōngchéngshī)(nóngmín)

（律师） （物理学家） （工会 工作者）

(lǜshī)(wùlǐ xuéjiā) (gōnghuì gōngzuòzhě)

（工人） （新闻 工作者）。

(gōngrén) (xīnwén gōngzuòzhě).

We're members of a (concert) (science) (sports)
(students) (trade) delegation.

我们 是 （音乐） （科学） （体育） （学生）

Wǒmen shì (yīnyuè) (kēxué) (tǐyù) (xuéshēng)

（贸易） 代表 团 的 团员。

(màoyì) dàibiǎotuán de tuányuán.

We're on a United Nations (agricultural study mission from FAO)(child health mission from WHO)

(student exchange programme from UNESCO).

我们 是 联合国 （粮 农 组织 农业
Wǒmen shì Liánhéguó (Liángnóng Zǔzhī nóngyè
考察 团） （世界 卫生 组织 儿童
kǎochá tuán) (Shìjiè Wèishēng Zǔzhī értóng
保健 代表团） （教科文 组织 学生
bǎojiàn dàibiǎotuán) (Jiāokēwén Zǔzhī xuésheng
交换 计划 团)的 成员。
jiàohuàn jìhuà tuán) de chéngyuán.

I don't speak Chinese.

我 不 会 讲 中国 话。
Wǒ bú huì jiǎng Zhōngguó huà.

But (Mr)(Mrs)(Miss) … does.

但是 … （先生） （夫人） （女士） 会。
Dànshì… (xiānsheng) (fūrén) (nǚshì) huì.

Can you speak (English) (French) (German)
(Japanese)?

您 会 讲 （英语）（法语）（德语）（日语）吗？
Nín huì jiǎng (Yīngyǔ) (Fǎyǔ) (Déyǔ) (Rìyǔ) ma?

I only speak (Spanish) (Arabic).

我 只会 讲 （西班牙语） （阿拉伯语）。
Wǒ zhǐ huì jiǎng (Xībānyáyǔ) (Ālābóyǔ).

This is my first trip to China.

这 是 我第一次来 中国。
Zhè shì wǒ dìyī cì lái Zhōngguó.

10

I would like to learn to (speak) (read) Chinese.

我 想 学 （讲） （看） 中文。

Wǒ xiǎng xué（jiǎng）（kàn）Zhōngwén.

I can read Chinese but cannot speak much.

我 能 看 中文， 但是 不 大 会 讲。

Wǒ néng kàn Zhōngwén，dànshì bú dà huì jiǎng.

Do you understand what I'm saying?

您 懂 我 在 讲 什么 吗?

Nín dǒng wǒ zài jiǎng shénme ma?

Yes，I do. No，I don't.

我 懂。 我 不 懂。

Wǒ dǒng. Wǒ bù dǒng.

I understand (less than half) (about half) (almost all).

我 能 听懂 （不到一半儿） （大约一半儿）

Wǒ néng tīngdǒng（búdàoyíbànr）（dàyuē yíbànr）.

（绝大 部分）。

（jué dà bùfen）.

Would you please repeat that?

请 您 再 说 一遍， 好 吗?

Qǐng nín zài shuō yíbiàn，hǎo ma?

Please tell me what that says.

请 您 告诉 我那儿写 的 是 什么。

Qǐng nín gàosu wǒ nàr xiě de shì shénme.

11

What does this word mean?

这个 字 是 什么 意思？

Zhège zì shì shénme yìsi?

How do you (pronounce) (write) this word?

这个 字 怎么 （念） （写）？

Zhège zì zěnme (niàn) (xiě)?

How old are you?

您多大岁数啦？

Nín duō dà suìshu la?

Are you married?

您结婚了吗？

Nín jiéhūnle ma?

Yes. And I have a (child) (two children). No, not yet.

结了。我 已经 有了（一个小孩儿） （两个

Jiéle. Wǒ yǐjing yǒule (yíge xiǎoháir) (liǎngge

小孩儿）。

xiǎoháir).

还没有。

Hái méiyǒu.

Boy or girl? How old?

是 男孩儿,还是 女孩儿？几岁 了？

Shì nánháir, háishì nǚháir? Jǐsuì le?

What are the members of your family?

您　家里有　什么　人?

Nín jiā li yǒu shénme rén?

There are ... (mother) (father) (sister) (brother)
(grandmother) (grandfather).

我　家里有　（母亲）　（父亲）（姐妹）（哥哥）

Wǒ jiā li yǒu…(mǔqīn) (fùqīn) (jiěmèi) (gēge)

（弟弟）（奶奶）（外祖母）　（爷爷）（外祖父）。

(dìdi)(nǎinai)(wàizǔmǔ)* (yéye) (wàizǔfù)*.

I'm a Moslem.

我　是 穆斯林。

Wǒ shì Mùsīlín.

Are you of the (Han) (Hui) (Mongolian) (Ti-
betan) (Miao) (Yi) (Zhuang) (Dai) (Uygur) na-
tionality?

您　是　（汉族）　（回族）　（蒙古族）　（藏族）

Nín shì (Hànzú)(Huízú)(Měnggǔzú)(Zàngzú)

（苗族）　　（彝族）　　（壮族）　　（傣族）

(Miáozú)　(Yízú)　(Zhuàngzú)　(Dǎizú)

（维吾尔族）吗?

(Wéiwúěrzú) ma?

---

* Refers to the maternal grandmother and grandfather.

13

How many nationalities are there in China?

中国　　有　多少　个　民族？

Zhōngguó yǒu duōshǎo ge mínzú?

There are over fifty.

有　五十　多　个。

Yǒu wǔshí duō gè.

Where do you work?

您　在　哪儿　工作？

Nín zài nǎr gōngzuò?

What do you study? Where?

您　学　什么？　在　哪儿？

Nín xué shénme? Zài nǎr?

I'm a (carpenter) (construction worker) (fitter) (hairdresser) (mechanic) (miner) (orchestra conductor) (tailor) (truck driver, bus driver, taxi driver).

我　是　（木工）　（建筑　工人）　　（钳工）

Wǒ shì（mùgōng）（jiànzhù gōngrén）（qiángōng）

（理发师）（机械师）　（矿工）　　（乐队　指挥）

（lǐfàshī）（jīxièshī）（kuànggōng）（yuèduì zhǐhuī）

（裁缝）　（卡车司机，　公共　汽车 司机，出租

（cáifeng）（kǎchēsījī，gōnggòng qìchē sījī，chūzū

汽车　司机）。

qìchē sījī）.

14

I'm a (foreman) (manager) (technician) (designer).

我 是(工长) (经理) (技术员) (设计师)。

Wǒ shì (gōngzhǎng)(jīnglǐ)(jìshùyuán)(shèjìshī).

I'm a (librarian) (office worker) (public relations worker) (salesperson) (secretary).

我 是 (图书 管理员) (职员) (对外

Wǒ shì (túshū guǎnlǐyuán) (zhí yuán) (duìwài

联 络员) (推销员) (秘书)。

liánluòyuán) (tuīxiāoyuán) (mìshū).

Happy (New Year) (birthday) (Spring Festival) (National Day)!

(新年) (生日) (春节) (国庆) 快乐!

(Xīnnián) (shēngrì) (Chūnjié) (Guóqìng)kuàilè!

Cheers!

干杯!

Gānbēi!

I propose a toast to the friendship between the people of our two countries.

我 建议 为 我们 两 国 人民 的 友谊

Wǒ jiànyì wèi wǒmen liǎng guó rénmín de yǒuyì

干杯。

gānbēi.

A toast to the successful cultural exchange between China and···!

为 中 ··· 文化 交流 事业 的 成功

Wèi Zhōng···wénhuà jiāoliú shìyè de chénggōng

干杯!

gānbēi!

Here's to your (health) (happiness) (success)!

祝 您 (你们) （健康） （幸福）

Zhù nín (nǐmen-pl.) (jiànkāng) (xìngfú)

（成功）!

(chénggōng)!

I wish you success in your modernization programme.

祝 你们 实现 现代化。

Zhù nǐmen shíxiàn xiàndàihuà.

Thank you for your gift.

谢谢 您 (你们) 的 礼物。

Xièxie nín (nǐmen) de lǐwù.

Thank you for your warm hospitality.

谢谢 您 (你们)的 热情 招待。

Xièxie nín nǐmen de rèqíng zhāodài.

Not at all.

不 要 客气。

Bú yào kèqi.

Please come in.

请　进。

Qǐngjìn.

Take off your coat, please.

请　脱掉　　大衣。

Qǐng tuōdiào dàyi.

Please sit down.

请　坐。

Qǐng zuò.

Would you like tea?

您　喝　茶　吗？

Nín hē chá ma?

Do you smoke?

您　抽　烟　吗？

Nín chōu yān ma?

Will you come to my room after supper to discuss
(plans) (travel arrangements) (food)?

请　您　晚饭　后　到我　房间　来，　商

Qǐngnín wǎnfàn hòu dào wǒfángjiān lái, shāng-

量　一下（计划）（旅行　安排）（用餐）　的

liàng yíxià (jìhuà)(lǚxíng ānpái)(yòngcān) de

事情，好吗？

shìqing, hǎoma?

Shall I come at 7 or 7:30?

我 七点 钟 来 还 是 七点半 来？

Wǒ qīdiǎnzhōng lái háishì qīdiǎn bàn lái?

Better make it eight.

最 好 八点钟 来。

Zuì hǎo bādiǎnzhōng lái.

Do you know what the weather will be like tomorrow for our trip to the Great Wall?

您 知道 明天 我们 去 长 城 天气

Nín zhīdào míngtiān wǒmen qù Chángchéng tiānqì

会 怎么 样？

huì zěnmeyàng?

The weather forecast says it will be a fine day but a little cooler.

气象 预报 说 明天 是个 好天，

Qìxiàng yùbào shuō míngtiān shì ge hǎo tiān,

但是 稍 凉 快 一点儿。

dànshì shāo liángkuài yìdiǎnr.

Will it be windier on the Great Wall?

长 城 上 风 会 大 吗？

Chángchéng shang fēng huì dà ma?

Yes，it's windier，and also (cooler) (colder) up there. Blossom time is about two weeks later than

18

in the city.

对， 长 城　　 上　　 风 要　 大一点儿，而且

Duì, Chángchéng shàng fēng yào dà yìdiǎnr, érqiě

要　 凉快 （冷） 一点。　 开花　 的　 时间

yào liángkuài (lěng) yìdiǎnr. Kāihuā de shíjiān

要　 比城里　 晚　 两 个　 星期。

yào bǐ chénglǐ wǎn liǎng ge xīngqī.

2. HOTEL AND TRAVEL ARRANGEMENTS

住宿和旅行

Zhùsù hé Lǚxíng

A. At the Hotel

住 宿

Zhùsù

I need an interpreter.

我 需要 一位 翻译。

Wǒ xūyào yí wèi fānyì.

Where are we staying?

我们 住 在 哪个 旅馆？

Wǒmen zhù zài něige lǚguǎn?

Have you any (single) (double) rooms? With private bath (shower)?

有 （单人）（双人）　房间　吗?带　洗澡

Yǒu（dānrén）（shuāngrén）fángjiān ma?Dài xǐzǎo

间 （淋浴）吗?

jiān（línyù）ma?

What are the rates for the rooms?

房租　多少?

Fángzū duōshǎo?

Reserve a（room）（suite）for（me）（us），please.

请　给　我　（我们）　预订（个）（一套）　房间。

Qǐng gěi（wǒ）wǒmen yùdìng（ge）（yítào）fángjiān.

I plan to stay for（one day）（two days）（three weeks）.

我　计划　住(一天)　（两天）　（三个星期）。

Wǒ jìhuà zhù(yìtiān)（liǎngtiān）（sāngèxīngqī）.

Where shall I leave the key?

我　应该　把　钥匙　放　在　哪儿?

Wǒ yīnggāi bǎ yàoshi fàng zài nǎr?

At the desk on the floor.

放　在　您　住的那　层楼　的　服务台　上。

Fàng zài nín zhù de nà cénglóu de fúwùtái shang.

Can I get the *Xinhua News Bulletin* at the desk?

我　能　在　服务台　找　到《新华　电讯　稿》

Wǒ néng zài fúwùtái zhǎo dào Xīnhuá diànxùn gǎo

21

吗?

ma?

Yes. Sorry, no.

能。 对不起,那儿 没有。

Néng. Duìbùqǐ, nàr méiyǒu.

Where's the (lift) (staircase)?

电梯 (楼梯)在 哪儿?

Diàntī (lóutī) zài nǎr?

Just turn (left) (right).

往 (左) (右) 拐。

Wǎng (zuǒ) (yòu) guǎi.

Go straight ahead.

一直 往 前 走。

Yìzhí wǎng qián zǒu.

Please take my luggage to my room.

请 把 行李 送到 我 的 房间。

Qǐng bǎ xíngli sòngdào wǒ de fángjiān.

I want to make an outside call.

我 要 往 外边儿 打 个 电话。

Wǒ yào wǎng wàibiānr dǎ ge diànhuà.

Where's the (barber shop) (dining room) (service desk) (washroom)?

(理发馆) (餐厅) (服务台) (厕所)在 哪儿?

(Lǐfàguǎn) (cāntīng) (fúwùtái) (cèsuǒ) zài nǎr?

What are the meal hours?

什么　时间　开　饭？

Shénme shíjiān kāi fàn?

Breakfast at 8:00, lunch at 12:00 and dinner at 7:00.

早饭　八点，　午饭　十二点，　晚饭　七点。

Zǎofàn bādiǎn, wǔfàn shíèrdiǎn, wǎnfàn qīdiǎn.

When is the (bar) (banking office) (post office) (shopping counter) open?

（酒巴）（银行）　（邮局）（小卖部）　　几点　到

(Jiǔbā)(yínháng)(yóujú)(xiǎomàibù)　jǐdiǎn dào

几点　营业？

jǐdiǎn yíngyè?

（5:00—11:00 p.m.）（8:00 a.m.—5:00 p.m.） （9:00 a.m.—6:00 p.m.）

（下午　五　点　到　晚　十一　点）（早　八　点

(Xiàwǔ wǔdiǎn dào wǎn shíyidiǎn)(Zǎo bā-diǎn

到　下午　五　点）　（早　九点　到　下午

dào xiàwǔ wǔdiǎn）（Zǎo jiǔdiǎn dào xiàwǔ

六点）。

liùdiǎn).

Please send (breakfast) (lunch) (dinner) to my room. It's No. 345.

请 把（早饭）（午饭）（晚饭） 送到 我 的

Qǐng bǎ zǎofàn wǔfàn wǎnfàn sòngdào wǒ de

房间。 房间 号码儿 是 三 四 五。

fángjiān. Fángjiān hàomǎr shì sān-sì-wǔ.

When can I get my laundry back?

我 的 衣服 什么 时候 能 洗好？

Wǒde yīfu shénme shíhou néng xǐhǎo?

(This evening) (tomorrow noon).

（今天 晚上） （明天 中午）。

(Jīntiān wǎnshang) (míngtiān zhōngwǔ).

Do you need it right away?

您 马上 就 想 要 吗？

Nín mǎshàng jiù xiǎng yào ma?

Can I get (this zipper) (my shoes) (watch) (tape recorder) repaired?

能 把 （这个 拉锁）（我 的 鞋）（手 表）

Néng bǎ (zhège lāsuǒ) (wǒde xié) (shǒubiǎo)

（录音机）修理 一下 吗？

(lùyīnjī) xiūlǐ yíxià ma?

Please wake me up at (five) (quarter to six) (four thirty).

请 在 （五点） （差 一刻 六点） （四点半）

Qǐng zài (wǔdiǎn) (chà yíkè liùdiǎn) (sìdiǎnbàn)

叫 醒 我。

jiào xǐng wǒ.

I didn't sleep well last night. Can I change to an inside room?

夜里 我 没 睡 好。能 给 我 换 一个 靠

Yèli wǒ méi shuì hǎo. Néng gěi wǒ huàn yíge kào

里边 的 房间 吗?

lǐbiān de fángjiān ma?

Please bring an extra blanket.

请 再 给 我 一条 毯子。

Qǐng zài gěi wǒ yìtiáo tǎnzi.

Is this drinking water?

这 水 可以 喝 吗?

Zhè shuǐ kěyǐ hē ma?

Do not disturb.

请 勿 打扰。

Qǐng wù dǎrǎo.

Is there any mail for me?

有 我 的 信件 吗?

Yǒu wǒde xìnjiàn ma?

Has anyone called for me?

有 人 找 过 我 吗?

Yǒu rén zhǎoguo wǒ ma?

Did they leave any message?

他们　留下　什么　话儿　没有？

Tāmen liúxià shénme huàr méiyǒu?

I'm leaving (today) (tonight) (tomorrow) (day after tomorrow).

我　（今天）　（今晚）　（明天）　　（后天）　走。

Wǒ (jīntiān) (jīnwǎn) (míngtiān) (hòutiān) zǒu.

Can I pay my bill now?

我　现在　付　钱，好　吗？

Wǒ xiànzài fùqián, hǎo ma?

Where's the barber shop?

理发馆　在　哪儿？

Lǐfàguǎn zài nǎr?

I need a haircut, not too short.

我　要　理发，但是　不要　剪得　太　短。

Wǒ yào lǐfà, dànshì búyào jiǎnde tài duǎn.

I need a shave.

我　要　刮脸。

Wǒ yào guāliǎn.

I want a shampoo and set.

我　要　洗头　和　做头发。

Wǒ yāo xǐtóu hé zuòtóufa.

I want a shampo and trim. No set.

我 要 洗头和 剪短 一点儿。不做头发。

Wǒ yào xǐtóu hé jiǎnduǎn yìdiǎnr Bú zuòtóufa.

I (want)(do not want) quinine water (hair oil).

我 （要）（不要） 奎宁 水（发油）。

Wǒ (yào) (búyào) kuíníng shuǐ (fàyóu).

I'd like a cold wave.

我要冷烫。

Wǒ yào lěngtàng.

I need a manicure.

我 要 修 指甲。

Wǒ yào xiū zhījia.

How much does that come to?

一共 要 付 多少 钱？

Yígòng yào fù duōshǎo qián？

bangs , fringe	mirror
刘海儿	镜子
liúhǎir	**jìngzi**
comb	nail polish
梳子	指甲油
shūzi	**zhījia yóu**
hair-brush	scissors
头发刷子	剪子
tóufà shuāzi	**jiǎnzi**

27

hairpin

头发卡子

tóufa qiǎzi

waves

波浪

bōlàng

旅　行

Lǚxíng

What's our itinerary?

我们的　旅行　路线　是　什么？

Wǒmen de lǚxíng lùxiàn shì shénme?

Have you a city map?

您　有　市区　地图　吗？

Nín yǒu shìqū dìtú ma?

What cities will we visit?

我们　将　访问　哪些　城市？

Wǒmen jiāng fǎngwèn něixiē chéngshì?

We'll go first to ⋯ and then to ⋯ and you'll leave China at ⋯.

我们　将　先到⋯　然后　去⋯　最后

Wǒmen jiāng xiāndào⋯ ránhòu qù⋯zuìhòu

你们　从…　离开　中国。

nǐmen cóng… líkāi Zhōngguó.

Beijing	Ānshan
北京	鞍山
Běijīng	**Ānshān**
Changchun	Changsha
长春	长沙
Chángchūn	**Chángshā**
Chengdu	Chongqing
成都	重庆
Chéngdū	**Chóngqìng**
Dalian	Datong
大连	大同
Dàlián	**Dàtóng**
Fushun	Guangzhou
抚顺	广州
Fǔshùn	**Guǎngzhōu**
Guilin	Hangzhou
桂林	杭州
Guìlín	**Hángzhōu**
Harbin	Hefei
哈尔滨	合肥
Hā'ěrbīn	**Héféi**

Hohhot	Jilin
呼和浩特	吉林
Hūhéhàotè	**Jílín**
Jinan	Kunming
济南	昆明
Jǐnán	**Kūnmíng**
Lanzhou	Lhasa
兰州	拉萨
Lánzhōu	**Lāsà**
Luoyang	Nanchang
洛阳	南昌
Luòyáng	**Nánchāng**
Nanjing	Nanning
南京	南宁
Nánjīng	**Nánníng**
Qingdao	Shanghai
青岛	上海
Qīngdǎo	**Shànghǎi**
Shenyang	Shijiazhuang
沈阳	石家庄
Shěnyáng	**Shíjiāzhuāng**
Suzhou	Taiyuan
苏州	太原
Sūzhōu	**Tàiyuán**

Tianjin

天津

Tiānjīn

Wuxi

无锡

Wúxī

Xi'an

西安

Xī'ān

Zhengzhou

郑州

Zhèngzhōu

Wuhan

武汉

Wǔhàn

Urumqi

乌鲁木齐

Wūlǔmùqí

Yan'an

延安

Yán'ān

Any other places?

还 去 其它 地方 吗?

Hái qù qítā dìfāng ma?

How about summer resorts?

到 避暑 胜地 去 吗?

Dào bìshǔ shèngdì qù ma?

The trip will take you to ⋯

你们 这次 旅行 将 到⋯

Nǐmen zhècì lǚxíng jiāng dào……

I'd suggest a cruise on the Songhua River.

我 建议 游览 松花 江。

Wǒ jiànyì yóulǎn Sōnghuā Jiāng.

Beidaihe Beach   Chengde

北戴河 海滨   承德

Běidàihé hǎibīn   **Chéngdé**

Lushan   Taishan

庐山   泰山

Lúshān   **Tàishān**

Are we to see any other interesting places?

我们 还 去 看其它 名胜 地方 吗？

Wǒmen hái qù kàn qítā míngshèng dìfang ma?

Daqing Oilfield

大庆油田

Dàqìng Yóutián

Dunhuang Grottoes   yungang Grottoes

敦煌石窟   云岗石窟

Dūnhuáng Shíkū   **Yúngǎng Shíkū**

Xishuangbanna   Jinggang Mountains

西双版纳   井冈山

Xīshuāngbǎnnà   **Jǐnggēngshān**

Jingdezhen   Stone Forest

景德镇   石林

Jǐngdézhèn   **Shílín**

Are we going by train, plane or bus?

我们　　乘　火车，飞机,还　是　汽车　去？

Wǒmen chéng huǒchē,fēijī,háishi qìchē qù?

How long will we be on the way?

路　上　我们　要　花　多少　时间？

Lùshang wǒmen yào huā duōshǎo shíjiān?

When do we set out?

我们　几　点　钟　出发？

Wǒmen jǐdiǎn zhōng chūfā?

What shall I do about my luggage?

行李　怎么　办？

Xíngli zěnme bàn?

Leave it (outside your door)(at the hotel) (in the lobby).

放在　　（房间　门外）　　（旅馆　里)(旅馆

Fàngzài(fángjiān ménwài)(lǚguǎn lǐ)(lǚguǎn

大厅　　里）。

dàtīng lǐ).

Please check these pieces.

请　把这些　寄存　起来。

Qǐng bǎ zhèxiē jìcún qǐlái.

What's my luggage allowance?

我 可以　带　多少　行李？

Wǒ kěyǐ dài duōshǎo xíngli?

What's the rate for overweight?

超 重 行李 要 付 多少 钱？

Chāozhòng xíngli yào fù duōshǎo qián?

When does the train depart?

火车 几 点 钟 开？

Huǒchē jǐdiǎn zhōng kāi?

What's the plane's departure time?

飞机 几 点 钟 起飞？

Fēijī jǐdiǎn zhōng qǐfēi?

Can we fly today?

今天 能 飞行 吗？

Jīntiān néng fēixíng ma?

Is there a stop-over en route?

中 途 要 停 吗？

Zhōngtú yào tíng ma?

Have you a pill against (air)(car) sickness?

您 有 防治 （晕机） （晕车）的 药 吗？

Nín yǒu fángzhì(yùn jī)(yùn chē) de yào ma?

I'd like a (first-class) (second-class) seat (sleeper).

我 要 （软） （硬） 座 （卧铺）。

Wǒ yào (ruǎn) (yìng) zuò (wòpù).

Will we arrive on time?

我们　能　　准时　到　吗？

Wǒmen néng zhǔnshí dào ma?

That will depend on the weather.

那　要　看　天气　了。

Nà yào kàn tiānqi le.

The train is usually on time.

火车　一般　都能　　正点　　到达。

Huǒchē yìbān dōunéng zhèngdiǎn dàodá.

This luggage is mine.

这　是我的　行李。

Zhè shì wǒde xíngli.

Can I use a camera?

可以　拍照　吗？

Kěyǐ pāizhào ma?

These are my personal effects.

这些　是　我自己　用的　东西。

Zhèxiē shì wǒ zìjǐ yòngde dōngxi.

What items are duty-free?

什么　东西　是　免税的？

Shénme dōngxi shì miǎnshuì de?

How much duty do I have to pay?

我　应该　上　多少　税？

Wǒ yīnggāi shàng duōshǎo shuì？

I have a diplomatic pass.

我 有 免验 证件。

Wǒ yǒu miǎnyàn zhèngjiàn.

I have an import licence.

我 有 进口 许可证。

Wǒ yǒu jìnkǒu xǔkězhèng.

Is the inspection over？

检查 完 了 吗？

Jiǎnchá wán le ma？

Customs papers (inspector)

海关 证件 （检查员）

Hǎiguān zhèngjiàn（jiǎncháyuán）

Please tell me where the (Friendship Association)
(Friendship Store)(travel agency)(ticket office)
is.

请 问 （对外 友协） （友谊 商店）

Qǐng wèn（Duìwài Yǒuxié）（Yǒuyì Shāngdiàn）

（旅行社） （售票处） 在 哪儿？

（lǚxíngshè）（shòupiàochù）zài nǎr？

Will you get me a taxi to go to the (Beijing)(Qian-
men)(Nationalities) (Xinqiao) Hotel，please？

您 能 帮 我 要 辆 车 去 （北京）

Nín néng bāng wǒ yào liàng chē qù（Běijīng）

（前门）　　（民族）（新侨）　饭店　吗？

（Qiánmén）（Mínzú）（Xīnqiáo）Fàndiàn ma？

How do you get to the (Friendship Guest House)
(International Hostel) (West Garden Hotel)?

到　（友谊　宾馆）　（国际　公寓）　（西苑

Dào（Yǒuyì Bīnguǎn）（Guójì Gōngyù）（Xīyuán

饭店）　怎么　走？

Fàndiàn）zěnme zǒu？

Is this (Wanfujing Street)(Chang'an Avenue)?

这　是　（王府井）　（长安）大街　吗？

Zhè shì（Wángfǔjǐng）（Cháng'ān）Dàjiē ma？

How far is it to Liulichang Antiquities Street?

到　琉璃厂　有　多　远？

Dào Liúlichǎng yǒu duō yuǎn？

Ten minutes by car from the hotel.

从　旅馆　坐　小　汽车　去，要　十　分　钟。

Cóng lǚguǎn zuò xiǎo qìchē qù，yào shífēnzhōng.

How do I get there?

怎么　去？

Zěnme qù？

I'm staying at the ⋯ hotel.

我　住　在⋯　饭店。

Wǒ zhù zài⋯Fàndiàn.

Can you direct me there?

您 能 告诉 我 怎么 去 那儿 吗？

Nín néng gàosu wǒ zěnme qù nàr ma?

Does this lane lead to the main street?

这条 胡同 通 大街 吗？

Zhètiáo hútòng tōng dàjiē ma?

Where's the toilet?

厕所 在 哪儿？

Cèsuǒ zài nǎr?

What's the next stop?

下 一 站 是 什么 地方？

Xià yí zhàn shì shénme dìfang?

How long does the train stop here?

火车 在 这儿 停 多久？

Huǒchē zài zhèr tíng duōjiǔ?

Where's the dining car?

餐车 在 哪儿？

Cānchē zài nǎr?

Please bring (a cup)(two cups) of tea (orange juice).

请 拿 （一杯） （两杯） 茶 （桔子汁)来。

Qǐng ná (yìbēi) (liǎngbēi) chá (júzizhī) lái.

Where do you turn (on) (off) the (light) (fan)

(loudspeaker)?

（灯）（电扇）（喇叭）在哪儿（开）（关）?

(Dēng) (diànshàn)(lǎba) zài nǎr (kāi) (guān)?

How do you (shut) (open) the window?

窗　户　　怎么　（关上）　（打开）?

Chuānghu zěnme(guānshàng)(dǎkāi)?

Please put me off at the Tian'anmen stop.

到　　天安门　　时，请告诉　我　下　车。

Dào Tiān'ānmén shí，qǐng gàosu wǒ xià chē.

bus stop (terminal)	bridge
汽车　站　（终点站）	桥
qìchē zhàn (zhōngdiǎn zhàn)	**qiáo**
main street	pedestrian crossing
大街	人行横道
dàjiē	**rénxíng héngdào**
policeman	river
警察	河流
jǐngchá	**héliú**
side street	sidewalk
胡同	便道
hútòng	**biàndào**
square	waiting room
广场	候车室
guǎngchǎng	**hòuchēshì**

traffic lights
红绿灯
hóng-lǜdēng

airport
机场
jīchǎng

3. TELEPHONING，SENDING LETTERS AND CABLES
电话、寄信和电报
Diànhuà，Jìxìn hé Diànbào

When is the post office open?

邮局 什么 时间 营业？

Yóujú shénme shíjiān yíngyè?

I want to (make a long-distance phone call) (send a cable) (post a letter).

我 要（打 个 长途 电话） （拍个 电报）
（寄信）。

**Wǒ yào（dǎ ge chángtú diànhuà）（pāi ge diànbào）
（jìxìn）.**

Where can I buy postcards?

明 信 片 在哪儿 买？

Míngxìnpiàn zài nǎr mǎi?

What are the postal rates for (an airmail letter) (a postcard) (an ordinary letter) (printed matter)?

寄 （航空信） （明信片） （平信） （印刷

Jì（hángkōngxìn）（míngxìnpiàn）（píngxìn）（yìnshuā

品）要 多少 钱？

pǐn）yào duōshǎo qián?

How about a registered letter?

寄 挂号信 要 多少 钱？

Jì guàhàoxìn yào duōshǎo qián?

Internal，20 fen；external 50 fen.

国内 两毛，国际 五毛。

Guónèi liǎngmáo，guójì wǔmáo.

How do you write the address in Chinese?

中文 地址 怎么 写？

Zhōngwén dìzhǐ zěnme xiě?

I would like some sets of Chinese Commemorative stamps.

我 想 买 几套 中国 纪念 邮票。

Wǒ xiǎng mǎi jǐtào Zhōngguó jìniàn yóupiào.

What are the (domestic) (international) rates for parcels?

（国内）（国际）寄 邮包 要 多少 钱？

（Guónèi）（guójì）jì yóubāo yào duōshǎo qián?

When should it arrive?

应 该 什么 时候 到？

Yīnggāi shénme shíhou dào?

Please give me your phone number.

请 告诉 我 您的 电话 号码。

Qǐng gàosu wǒ nín de diànhuà hàomǎ.

Will you phone me?

您 给 我 打 个 电话， 好吗?

Nín gěi wǒ dǎ ge diànhuà, hǎo ma?

This is ··· speaking.

我 是···

Wǒ shì···

Can I speak to ···?

我 可以 和 ··· 讲话 吗?

Wǒ kěyǐ hé ··· jiǎnghuà ma?

Is there a phone nearby?

附近 有 电话 吗?

Fùjìn yǒu diànhuà ma?

When is the mail collected?

他们 几点 钟 来 开 邮箱?

Tāmen jǐdiǎnzhōng lái kāi yóuxiāng?

4. SIGHTSEEING AND VISITS
参观、游览 和 访问
Cānguān, Yóulǎn hé Fǎngwèn

A. General Expressions
一般用语
Yìbān Yòngyǔ

We'd like to see a (steel mill) (state farm) (watch factory).

我 们 想 参观 一个 （钢铁厂）

Wǒmen xiǎng cānguān yíge (gāngtiěchǎng)

（农 场） （手表 厂）。

(nóngchǎng) (shǒubiǎo chǎng).

We'd like to see a (nursery) (primary school) (teachers' college) (university).

我们 想 参观 一个 （托儿所） （小学）

Wǒmen xiǎng cānguān yíge (tuōérsuǒ)(xiǎoxué)

（师范　学院）（大学）。

shīfàn xuéyuàn）（dàxué).

We'd like to see a (Chinese traditional medicine institute) (scientific research institute).

我们　想　参观　一个　（中医　研究所）

Wǒmen xiǎng cānguān yíge（zhōngyī yánjiūsuǒ)

（科学　研究所）。

（kēxué yánjiūsuǒ).

We'd like to see what you're doing in (afforestation) (cancer prevention research) (farm mechanization) (fresh-water fish raising) (pollution control).

我　们　想　看看　你们　是　怎样　进行

Wǒmen xiǎng kànkan nǐmen shì zěnyàng jìnxíng

（植树　造林）（癌症　防治　研究）（农业

（zhíshù zàolín)（áizhèng fángzhì yánjiū)（nóngyè

机械化）（淡水　养鱼）（污染　控制）　的。

jīxièhuà)（dànshuǐ yǎngyú)（wūrǎn kòngzhì) de.

We'd like to see an operation under acupuncture anaesthesia.

我　们　想　看　看　用　针灸　麻醉　进行

Wǒmen xiǎng kànkan yòng zhēnjiǔ mázuì jìnxíng

45

的 手术。

de shǒushù.

I've really enjoyed the visit today!

今天 的 参观　非常 有 意思!

Jīntiān de cānguān fēicháng yǒu yìsi!

It's marvellous!

真好!

Zhēnhǎo!

The trip was very informative, though I'd still like to know how the secret entrance to the Ming Tombs was discovered.

这次 参观　非常　有 收获, 尽管 我

Zhècì cānguān fēicháng yǒu shōuhuò, jìnguǎn wǒ

还不 知道 十三陵　地下 宫陵 的 入口

háibù zhīdào Shísānlíng Dìxià Gōngdiàn de rùkǒu

是 怎么 发现 的。

shì zěnme fāxiàn de.

We've enjoyed our visit and look forward to coming again.

我 们 的 访问 很 愉快, 并 期待 着

Wǒmen de fǎngwèn hěn yúkuài, bìng qīdàizhe

以后 再来。

yǐhòu zàilái.

Thank you for showing us around your (factory) (farm).

谢谢 您 带 我们 参观 了 你们 的 （工厂） （农场）。

Xièxie nín dài wǒmen cānguānle nǐmen de (gōng-chǎng)(nóngchǎng).

B. Industry

工业

Gōngyè

We'd like to talk with the (manager) (chief engineer) (shop foreman) (a worker).

我们 想 和 （厂长） （总 工程师）

Wǒmen xiǎnghé(chǎngzhǎng)(zǒng gōngchéngshī)

（车间 主任） （一个 工人） 谈 谈。

(chējiān zhǔrèn) (yíge gōngrén) tántan.

Do you have a trade union?

你们 有 工会 组织 吗？

Nǐmen yǒu gōnghuì zǔzhī ma?

How are (factory) (shop) (trade union) leaders

47

elected?

（工厂）　　（车间）（工会）领导　是　怎么
(Gōngchǎng) (chējiān) (gōnghuì) lǐngdǎo shì zěnme

选举　的？

xuǎnjǔ de?

What workers' benefits does this factory provide?

这个　工　厂　工　人　都　享受　什么

Zhège gōngchǎng gōngrén dōu xiǎngshòu shénme

福利　待遇？

fúlì dàiyù?

What about labour protection?

劳　动　保护　包括　哪些　项目？

Láodòng bǎohù bāokuò něixiē xiàngmù?

What's the wage scale?

工资　分　多少　级？

Gōngzi fēn duōshǎo jí?

How about the workers' recreational facilities?

工　人　们　　有　哪些　文娱　设施？

Gōngrénmen yǒu něixiē wényù shèshī?

At what age do workers retire?

工　人　多大　岁数　退休？

Gōngrén duōdà suìshù tuìxiū?

How about pensions?

退休金　是　多少？

Tuìxiūjīn shì duōshǎo?

How about sick leave?

病假　有　什么　规定？

Bìngjià yǒu shénme guīdìng?

Suppose a worker is injured on the job?

出　现　工伤　时　怎么　办？

Chūxiàn gōngshāng shí zěnme bàn?

Do workers have a voice in management?

工　人　参　加　工厂　管理　吗？

Gōngrén cānjiā gōngchǎng guǎnlǐ ma?

What's your annual (production) (production value) (cost of production)?

你们　厂　每　年　（产量）（产值）

Nǐmen chǎng měinián（chǎnliàng）（chǎnzhí）

（生产　成本）是　多少？

（shēngchǎn chéngběn）shì duōshǎo?

How many are there on the payroll here? How many women?

全厂　有　多少　职工？　有　多少

Quánchǎng yǒu duōshǎo zhígōng? Yǒu duōshǎo

女工？

nǚgōng?

Where are these machines made?

这些 机器 是哪儿 制造的？

Zhèxiē jīqì shì nǎr zhìzào de?

What fuel is used?

使 用 什么 燃料？

Shǐyòng shénme ránliào?

Where do you get funds for developing production?

发 展 生 产 的 资金 从 哪儿 来？

Fāzhǎn shēngchǎn de zījīn cóng nǎr lái?

Do you have the bonus system here?

你们 实行 奖金 制度 吗？

Nǐmen shíxíng jiǎngjīn zhìdù ma?

C. Agriculture

农业

Nóngyè

How is the administration in a （township）
（village）organized?

（乡） （村） 政府 是 怎样 组织的？

（Xiāng）（cūn）zhèngfǔ shì zěnyàng zǔzhī de?

How are the leaders elected?

干部 是 怎样 选举的？

Gànbù shì zěnyàng xuǎnjǔ de?

What's the term?

多 长 时间 选举 一次？

Duōcháng shíjiān xuǎnjǔ yícì?

How is the income distributed?

收入 是 怎样 分配的？

Shōurù shì zěnyàng fēnpèi de?

How much land do the farmers have?

农 民 有 多少 地？

Nóngmín yǒu duōshǎo dì?

Are the farmers allowed to engage in household sideline production?

农 民 搞 家庭 副业 吗？

Nóngmín gǎo jiātíng fùyè ma?

Do you hold village fairs?

你们 有 自由 市场 吗？

Nǐmen yǒu zìyóu shìchǎng ma?

Is there any regulation on prices?

对 价格 有 什么 规定 吗？

Duì jiàgé yǒu shénme guīdìng ma?

What's your main product? Others? How do you

market them?

你们 主要 生产 什么？ 还 生产

Nǐmen zhǔyào shēngchǎn shénme?Hái shēngchǎn

别的 吗？ 怎么 销售？

biéde ma?Zěnme xiāoshòu?

How much agricultural tax do you pay?

你们 要 付 多少 农业 税？

Nǐmen yào fù duōshǎo nóngyèshuì?

What are you doing in farmland capital construc-tion?

你们 在 搞 什么 农田 基本 建设？

Nǐmen zài gǎo shénme nóngtián jīběn jiànshè?

What's the farmers' average annual income?

农 民 平均 每年 收入 多少？

Nóngmín píngjūn měinián shōurù duōshǎo?

How much work is done by machine in your vil-lage?

你们 村 机械化 达到了 什么 程度？

Nǐmen cūn jīxièhuà dádàole shénme chéngdù?

How is the production plan made?

生产 计划 是 怎么 制定 的？

Shēngchǎn jìhuà shì zěnme zhìdìng de?

D. Medicine and Education
卫生和教育
Wèishēng hé Jiàoyù

How many departments are there in this hospital?
How many beds?

这所 医院 有 多少 个 科室?有 多少
Zhèsuǒ yīyuàn yǒu duōshǎo ge kēshì?Yǒu duōshǎo
个 床位?
ge chuángwèi?

That doctor is very skilful. Where did he graduate?

那位 医生 医术 高明, 他是 哪所 大学
Nàwèi yīshēng yīshù gāomíng,tā shì nǎsuǒ dàxué
毕业 的?
bìyè de?

Are you attached to a medical college?

你们 是 医学院 的 附属 医院 吗?
Nǐmen shì yīxuéyuàn de fùshǔ yīyuàn ma?

Is acupuncture (anaesthesia) (treatment) used in
your hospital?

你们　　医院　　　使用　　针灸　（麻醉）（治疗）
Nǐmen yīyuàn shǐyòng zhēnjiǔ(mázuì)(zhìliáo)

吗？

ma?

How do you combine Chinese traditional and Western medicine in clinical practice?

在　临床　　实践　　中，你们　　是　怎样
Zài línchuáng shíjiàn zhōng，nǐmen shì zěnyàng

实行　中　西　医　结合　的？
shíxíng zhōng xī yī jiéhé de？

What's the school age here?

入学　年龄　是　几岁？
Rùxué niánlíng shì jǐsuì？

Is school attendance compulsory?

每个　儿童　都　必须　上学　吗？
Měige értóng dōu bìxū shàngxué ma？

How many subjects are taught in (primary schools) (high schools)?

（小学）　　（中学）里　有几门儿　课？
(Xiǎoxué)(zhōngxué)lǐ yǒu jǐménr kè？

Do you teach any foreign languages in your school?

你们　学　校　教　外语　吗？
Nǐmen xuéxiào jiāo wàiyǔ ma？

Does the school plan activities for students on holidays?

你们　学校　在　假期里给　学生　安排
Nǐmen xuéxiào zài jiàqī lǐ gěi xuéshēng ānpái
什么　活动　吗？
shénme huódòng ma?

When does a student begin to specialize in a subject?

学生　　几年级　开始　进行　专业　训练？
Xuéshēng jǐniánjí kāishǐ jìnxíng zhuānyè xùnliàn?

How long is the university course?

大学　学制　是　几年？
Dàxué xuézhì shì jǐnián?

How do you test your students when they graduate?

学生　毕业　时　进行　什么样　的　考试？
Xuéshēng bìyè shí jìnxíng shénmeyàng de kǎoshì?

What's the ratio between students enrolled and those who apply?

报名的　和　录取的　学生　之间　比例　是
Bàomíngde hé lùqǔde xuéshēng zhījiān bǐlì shì
多少？
duōshǎo?

Are students allowed to marry during their studies?

学 生 学习 期间 可以 结婚 吗?

Xuéshēng xuéxí qījiān kěyǐ jiéhūn ma?

Is there any dropout among your students?

你们 的 学生 有 中途 退学的 吗?

Nǐmen de xuéshēng yǒu zhōngtú tuìxué de ma?

How do they find jobs upon graduation?

毕业 后 学生 怎样 找 工作?

Bìyè hòu xuéshēng zěnyàng zhǎo gōngzuò?

E. Miscellaneous

其它

Qítā

When was the (Great Wall) (Imperial Palace) (Summer Palace) (Art Gallery) built?

(长城) (故宫) (颐和园) (美术馆)

(Chángchéng)(Gùgōng)(Yíhéyuán)(Měishùguǎn)

是 什么 时候 修建的?

shì shénme shíhou xiūjiàn de?

Is Beijing Zoo the largest in the country?

北京　动物园　是　全国　最大的　吗？

Běijīng Dòngwùyuán shì quánguó zuìdàde ma？

How are the pandas doing?

大　熊猫　长得　好　吗？

Dàxióngmāo zhǎngde hǎo ma？

Can we see them?

能　看看　它们　吗？

Néng kànkan tāmen ma？

How long will we spend in the (North Sea Park)
(Fragrance Hill Park) (Temple of Heaven) (Coal
Hill Park)?

我　们　在　（北海　公园）　　　（香山

Wǒmen zài（Běihǎi Gōngyuán）（Xiāngshān

公园）　　　（天坛　公园）　　　（景山

Gōngyuán）（Tiāntán Gōngyuán）（Jǐngshān

公园）　呆　多久？

Gōngyuán）dāi duōjiǔ？

Can we take pictures in the Ming Tombs Under-
ground Palace?

可以　在　十三陵　地下　宫殿　拍照　吗？

Kěyǐ zài Shísānlíng Dìxià Gōngdiàn pāizhào ma？

5. RESTAURANTS
饭馆
Fànguǎn

We'd like to go out for a meal.

我们　想　到　外边　去　吃饭。

Wǒmen xiǎng dào wàibiān qù chīfàn.

What restaurant would you suggest?

您　建议　我们　去　哪个　饭馆儿?

Nín jiànyì wǒmen qù nǎige fànguǎnr?

Where can we get roast Beijing duck?

在哪儿可以　吃到　北京　烤鸭?

Zài nǎr kěyǐ chīdào Běijīng kǎoyā?

At the Hepingmen Roast Beijing Duck Restaurant.

在　　和平门　　烤鸭店。

Zài Hépíngmén Kǎoyādiàn.

What's the price per person?

每个　人　要　花　多少　钱?

Měige rén yào huā duōshǎo qián?

Have you a table vacant?

有 空 位 子 吗？

Yǒu kòng wèizi ma?

Have you a menu in English?

有 英文 的 菜单儿 吗？

Yǒu Yīngwén de càidānr ma?

What's your specialty?

什么 是 你们 的 特殊 风味儿 菜？

Shénme shì nǐmen de tèshū fēngwèir cài?

What soft drinks have you got — (orange) (mineral) water?

你们 有 什么 饮料 （桔子水） （矿 泉

Nǐmen yǒu shénme yǐnliào(júzishuǐ)(kuàngquán

水)？

shuǐ)?

Do you have iced (beer)(champagne)(Coca-Cola)?

你们 有 冰镇 （啤酒） （香槟酒） （可口

Nǐmen yǒu bīngzhèn (píjiǔ)(xiāngbīnjiǔ) (kěkǒu-

可乐） 吗？

kělè)ma?

I want a bottle of (Maotai) (brandy) (red grape wine) (dry red grape wine).

我 要 一瓶 （茅台） （白兰地） （甜 葡萄酒）

Wǒ yào yìpíng (Máotái)(báilándì)(tián pútáo jiǔ)

59

（干　红　葡萄酒）。

（gānhóng pútáo jiǔ）.

I'd like a glass of （dry white grape wine）（rum）
（liqueur）.

我　要　一杯　（干白　葡萄酒）（甜酒）　（烈性

Wǒ yào yìbēi （gānbái pútáo jiǔ）（tiánjiǔ）（lièxìng

甜酒）。

tiánjiǔ）.

I'm a vegetarian. I eat eggs, beancurd and dairy
products.

我　吃　素。我　吃　鸡蛋、豆腐　和　奶制品。

Wǒ chī sù. Wǒ chī jīdàn, dòufu hé nǎizhìpǐn.

I'm a Moslem.

我　是　穆斯林。

Wǒ shì Mùsīlín.

I'd like （Chinese）（Western）food.

我　要　（中）（西）　餐。

Wǒ yào （Zhōng）（Xī）cān.

I （like）（do not like）hot, peppery food.

我　（爱吃）　（不爱吃）辣的　东西。

Wǒ （àichī）（bú àichī）là de dōngxi.

What fish dishes do you have?

你们　有　什么　鱼　做的　菜？

Nǐmen yǒu shénme yú zuò de cài?

I want (fried) (broiled) (baked) fish (fish aspic).

我 要 （炸）（烧）（烤）鱼（鱼冻）。

Wǒ yào (zhá) (shāo) (kǎo) yú (yúdòng).

What kind of (chicken) (duck) do you have?

你们 有 什么 （鸡）（鸭）做的 菜？

Nǐmen yǒu shénme (jī) (yā) zuò de cài?

What kind of bread do you have?

你们 有 什么 面包？

Nǐmen yǒu shénme miànbāo?

We'll have two orders of (steak) (roast beef) (roast pork).

我们 要 两份儿 （牛排） （烤牛肉） （烤

Wǒmen yào liǎngfènr (niúpái) (kǎo niúròu) (kǎo

猪肉）。

zhūròu).

We'd like some mutton skewers (with) (without) red pepper.

我们 要 点儿（辣的）（不辣的）羊肉 串儿。

Wǒmen yào diǎnr (làde) (búlàde) yángròu chuànr.

What (salad) (cold dish) do you have?

你们 有 什么 （撒拉菜） （冷盘儿）？

Nǐmen yǒu shénme (sālà cài) (lěngpánr)?

Please bring us some (fresh cucumbers) (canned peas) (radishes) (tomatoes) (carrots).

请 给 我们 一些 (生 黄瓜) (罐头

Qǐng gěi wǒmen yìxiē (shēng huángguā)(guàntóu

豌豆) (水萝卜) (西红柿) (胡萝卜)。

wāndòu)(shuǐluóbo)(xīhóngshì)(húluóbo).

What will you have ,black tea or coffee?

您 想 喝 什么，红茶 还是 咖啡？

Nín xiǎng hē shénme,hóngchá háishì kāfēi?

Would you pass me the (milk) (pepper)(salt), please.

请 把 (牛奶)(胡椒)(盐)递给 我。

Qǐng bǎ (niúnǎi)(hújiāo)(yán) dì gěi wǒ.

Can we get (fresh fruit) (cake) (biscuits)?

有 (新鲜 水果) (点心) (饼干) 吗？

Yǒu (xīnxiān shuǐguǒ)(diǎnxīn)(bǐnggān) ma?

How is your appetite today?

您 今天 胃口 好 吗？

Nín jīntiān wèikǒu hǎo ma?

Do you like the food?

您 爱 吃 这个 吗？

Nín ài chī zhège ma?

Yes. It's delicious.

爱吃。很 好 吃。

Àichī. Hěn hǎo chī.

It's not bad.

不错。

Búcuò.

The cooking is very good.

你们 的 烹调 技术 很好。

Nǐmen de pēngtiáo jìshù hěnhǎo.

I'd like to see the chef.

我 想 见见 厨师。

Wǒ xiǎng jiànjian chúshī.

Please lay another place. Please give me (us) a ···

请 再 给 我们 一份儿 餐具。请给 我

Qǐng zài gěi wǒmen yífènr cānjù. Qǐng gěi wǒ

（我们） 一个···

（wǒmen) yíge···

dinner plate	egg-cup
菜盘儿	蛋杯
càipánr	**dànbēi**
fork	knife
叉子	刀子
chāzi	**dāozi**

saucer	soup plate
茶碟儿	汤盘儿
chádiér	**tāngpánr**
table spoon	tea spoon
汤匙	茶匙
tāngchí	**cháchí**
tumbler	wine glass
水杯	酒杯
shuǐbēi	**jiǔbēi**

Miscellaneous Foods and Terms

其它　食品　和　名称

Qítā Shípǐn hé Míngchēng

apple pie	bamboo shoots
苹果　　馅儿饼	笋
píngguǒ xiànrbǐng	**sǔn**
bread，brown	bread，white
黑　面包	白　面包
hēi miànbāo	**bái miànbāo**
butter	cheese
黄油	干酪
huángyóu	**gānlào**
cocoa	dumpling
可可	饺子
kěkě	**jiǎozi**

egg, fried	egg, hard-boiled
荷包蛋	熟 鸡蛋
hébāodàn	**shú jīdàn**
egg, scrambled	egg, soft-boiled
炒 鸡蛋	半熟 的 鸡蛋
chǎo jīdàn	**bànshú de jīdàn**
fruit cocktail	fruit, fresh
什锦 水果	新鲜 水果
shíjǐn shuǐguǒ	**xīnxiān shuǐguǒ**
apple	banana
苹果	香蕉
píngguǒ	**xiāngjiāo**
peach	orange
桃	桔子
táo	**júzi**
pear	watermelon
梨	西瓜
lí	**xīguā**
garlic	grilled (beef) (mutton)
大蒜	铁扒(牛肉) (羊肉)
dàsuàn	**tiěpá (niúròu) (yángròu)**
ham	ice-cream (soda)
火腿	冰激凌 (汽水儿)
huǒtuǐ	**bīngjilíng (qìshuǐr)**

jam, fruit

果酱

guǒjiàng

marmalade

桔子酱

júzijiàng

noodles with hot sauce

辣 酱 面

làjiàngmiàn

scallions, onions

葱 （葱头）

cōng（cōngtóu）

powdered meat

肉松

ròusōng

rice, fried

炒饭

chǎofàn

sandwich

三明治

sānmíngzhì

chocolate

巧克力

qiǎokèlì

liver

肝

gān

noodles with sauce

炸 酱 面

zhájiàngmiàn

omelette

煎蛋卷儿

jiāndànjuǎnr

pepper oil

辣椒油

làjiāoyóu

preserved duck egg

松花 蛋

sōnghuādàn

rice, steamed

米饭

mǐfàn

soy sauce

酱油

jiàngyóu

sponge cake

蛋糕

dàngāo

spring roll

春卷儿

chūnjuǎnr

steak

牛排

niúpái

vinegar

醋

cù

breakfast

早饭

zǎofàn

supper (dinner)

晚饭　（正餐）

wǎnfàn（zhèngcān）

snack

快餐

kuàicān

cocktail party

鸡尾　酒会

jīwěi jiǔhuì

sugar

糖

táng

vegetables，green

蔬菜

shūcài

water，cold，boiled

凉开　水

liángkāishuǐ

lunch

午饭

wǔfàn

refreshments

茶点

chádiǎn

buffet

冷餐

lěngcān

banquet

宴会

yànhuì

6. SHOPS
商店
Shāngdiàn

A. Jewellery, Arts and Crafts
珠宝、美术工艺品
Zhūbǎo, Měishù Gōngyìpǐn

Is there an arts and crafts (shop) near here?

附近 有 美术工艺品 （商店） 吗？

Fùjìn yǒu měishù gōngyìpǐn (shāngdiàn) ma?

Where can I get an embroidered tablecloth?

在 哪儿 能 买到 绣花 桌布？

Zài nǎr néng mǎidào xiùhuā zhuōbù?

Please show me some (jade jewellery) (bamboo chopsticks) (sandalwood fans) (snuff bottles).

请 拿 给 我 一些 （玉石 珠宝）（竹 筷子）

Qǐng ná gěi wǒ yìxiē (yùshí zhūbǎo) (zhúkuàizi)

（檀香　　木扇子）（鼻烟壶儿）看看。

（tánxiāngmù shànzi）（bíyānhúr）kànkan.

I'd like to see some (ivory) (wood) (jet) (jade-stone) carvings.

我　想　看看　　（象牙）（木）（墨玉）（玉石）

Wǒ xiǎng kànkan（xiàngyá）（mù）（mòyù）（yùshí）

雕刻。

diāokè.

Please show me a (vase) (dinner-set) (coffee-service) (tea-cup) (tea-service).

请　给　我　拿一个（花瓶）一套（餐具）一套

Qǐng gěi wǒ ná yíge（huāpíng）yítào（cānjù）yítào

（咖啡具）一个（茶杯）一套（茶具）。

（kāfēijù）yíge（chábēi）yítào（chájù）.

I want to buy a (bowl) (dish) (coffee-pot) (plate) (teapot) with Chinese designs.

我　要买　一个带　中　国　图案的（碗）

Wǒ yàomǎi yíge dài Zhōngguó túàn de（wǎn）

（碟子）（咖啡壶）（大盘子）（茶壶）。

（diézi）（kāfēihú）（dàpánzi）（cháhú）.

agate   amber

玛瑙   琥珀

mǎnǎo   **hǔpò**

bambooware	batik
竹器	蜡染 印花布
zhúqì	**làrǎn yìnhuābù**
boxes, nest of	bracelet
套盒	手镯
tàohé	**shǒuzhuó**
cloisonné	carpet
景泰蓝	地毯
jǐngtàilán	**dìtǎn**
cushion	diamond
垫子	钻石
diànzi	**zuànshí**
embroidery	fan
刺绣	扇子
cìxiù	**shànzi**
jewellery	jewel case
珠宝	手饰盒
zhūbǎo	**shǒushìhé**
lacquerware	lacquer, carved
漆器	雕漆
qīqì	**diāoqī**
necklace	paper cut
项链	剪纸
xiàngliàn	**jiǎnzhǐ**

pearl (cultured)   porcelain

珍珠（养珠）   磁器

zhēnzhū（yǎngzhū）   **cíqì**

pottery   signet , ring

陶器   印章   戒指

táoqì   **yìnzhāng jièzhi**

tapestry   tea (smoking) set

挂毯   茶（烟）具

guàtǎn   **chá（yān）jù**

Is this an original painting?

这幅 画 是 原作 吗？

Zhèfú huà shì yuánzuò ma?

What's the theme of this painting?

这幅 画 的题材 是 什么？

Zhèfú huà de tícái shì shénme?

Could you please tell something about the painter?

您 是否 给 我们 介绍 一下 这位 画家

Nín shìfǒu gěi wǒmen jièshào yíxià zhèwèi huàjiā

的 情况？

de qíngkuàng?

I'm very interested in Chinese （paintings）
(murals) (posters) (stone rubbings).

我 对 中国   （彩墨画 ）（壁画） （招贴画）

Wǒ duì Zhōngguó（cǎimòhuà）（bìhuà）（zhāotiēhuà）

（拓碑）很 感 兴趣。
(tàbēi)hěn gǎn xìngqu.

Are these reproductions of the Tang Dynasty (figure paintings) (sculptures)?

这些 是 唐朝 （人物画）（雕塑） 的
Zhèxiē shì Tángcháo (rénwùhuà)(diāosù) de

复制品 吗？
fùzhìpǐn ma?

cartoon	flower and bird
漫画	花鸟
mànhuà	**huāniǎo**
graphic art	landscape
版画	风景(山水)画
bǎnhuà	**fēngjǐng (shānshuǐ)huà**
New Year picture	oil painting
年画	油画
niánhuà	**yóuhuà**
painter	painting in Chinese ink
画家	水墨画
huàjiā	**shuǐmòhuà**
picture story	pigments
连环画	颜料
liánhuánhuà	**yánliào**

72

poster

招贴画

zhāotiēhuà

sketch

速写

sùxiě

water-colour painting

水彩画

shuǐcǎihuà

sculptor

雕塑家

diāosùjiā

still life

静物画

jìngwùhuà

woodcut

木刻

mùkè

B. Textiles
纺织品
Fǎngzhīpǐn

Please show me some (suit) (dress) material.

请 把（男）（女）衣料 拿 给 我 看 看。

Qǐ bǎ（nán）（nǚ）yīliào ná gěi wǒ kànkan.

I should like a (lighter) (darker) material, with (stripes) (checks).

我 要 颜色 （浅）（深） 一点儿的， 带（条儿）

Wǒ yào yánsè（qiǎn）（shēn）yìdiǎnr de, dài（tiáor）

73

(格儿)的 料子。

(gér)de liàozi.

Is this pure wool, or a mixture?

这 是 纯毛的， 还是 混纺的 料子？

Zhè shì chúnmáo de, háishì hùnfǎng de liàozi?

How wide is it?

有 多 宽？

Yǒu duō kuān?

What's the price per metre?

多 少 钱 一米？

Duōshǎo qián yì mǐ?

How many metres do I need for a dress for a large six-year-old?

一个 高个儿的六岁 孩子 做 一件 连衣裙

Yíge gāogèrde liùsuì háizi zuò yíjiàn liányīqún

需要 几米 料子？

xūyào jǐ mǐ liàozi?

Give me (two and a half) (three) metres.

我要 （两米半） （三米）。

Wǒ yào (liǎngmǐbàn)(sānmǐ).

Is this silk or rayon?

这 是 真丝，还是 人造丝？

Zhè shì zhēnsī, háishì rénzàosī?

What cotton prints have you?

你们　有　什么　　印花布？

Nǐmen yǒu shénme yìnhuābù?

Have you any other (colours) (patterns)?

你们　有　别的(颜色)　(花样)　吗？

Nǐmen yǒu biéde（yánsè）(huāyàng) ma?

Show me a (brighter) (softer) pattern.

给　我　拿一件　图案　(鲜艳)(素)一点儿的。

Gěi wǒ ná yíjiàn túàn（xiānyàn）(sù) yìdiǎnr de.

Please show me some men's (linen) (embroidered) handkerchiefs.

请　把　男的(麻)(刺绣)　手帕　拿给我

Qǐng bǎ nánde（má）(cìxiù) shǒupà ná gěi wǒ

看看。

kànkan.

Please show me some （ladies'）（men's）(children's) knitted underwear.

请　把　针织　(女)　(男)(儿童)　内衣　给

Qǐng bǎ zhēnzhī（nǚ）(nán)(értóng) nèiyī gěi

我 看看。

wǒ kànkan.

I want a swimming suit.

我　要　买　　游泳衣。

Wǒ yào mǎi yóuyǒngyī.

Do you have a (suit) (Chinese-style suit) to fit me?

你们 有 适合 我穿的 （西服） （中式

Nǐmen yǒu shìhé wǒ chuān de (xīfú) (zhōngshì

制服） 吗？

zhìfú) ma?

I'd like a (blouse) (skirt).

我 要 一件 （女衬衣） （裙子）。

Wǒ yào yíjiàn (nǚchènyī) (qúnzi).

I want a jacket for my five-year-old (son) (daughter).

我 要 五岁（男孩儿） （女孩儿） 穿的 上衣。

Wǒ yào wǔsuì (nánháir) (nǚháir) chuānde shàngyī.

Can I have an overcoat made here?

我 可以 在这儿 订做 一件 大衣 吗？

Wǒ kěyǐ zài zhèr dìng zuò yíjiàn dàyī ma?

Please show me a pattern book.

请 把 时装 样本 拿给 我 看看。

Qǐng bǎ shízhuāng yàngběn nágěi wǒ kànkan.

When will it be ready?

什么 时候 能 做好？

Shénme shíhou néng zuò hǎo?

Make it (tighter) (longer) (shorter) (wider).

做的 （瘦些） （长些） （短些） （宽些）。

Zuò de (shòuxiē) (chángxiē) (duǎnxiē) (kuānxiē).

blouse
女衬衣
nǚchènyī

button
钮扣儿
niǔkòur

coat（jacket）
外衣（上衣）
wàiyī（shàngyī）

denim
劳动布
láodòngbù

gauze
罗纱
luóshā

Orlon
腈纶
jīnglún

pocket
口袋儿（兜儿）
kǒudàir（dōur）

satin，figured
花缎
huāduàn

brocade
织锦缎
zhījǐnduàn

cashmere
开司米
kāisīmǐ

corduroy
灯心绒
dēngxīnróng

flannel
法兰绒
fǎlánróng

linen
麻布
mábù

overcoat
大衣
dàyī

satin
缎子
duànzi

shirt
男衬衣
nánchènyī

suit	skirt
制服	裙子
zhìfú	**qúnzi**
tweed	trousers
花呢	裤子
huāní	**kùzi**
vinylon	velvet
维尼纶	平绒
wéinílún	**píngróng**
woollen dacron	woollen goods
毛的良	呢绒织品
máodíliáng	**níróngzhīpǐn**

C. Furs
皮货
Píhuò

Have you any leather gloves?

有　皮　手套儿　吗？

Yǒu pí shǒutào ma?

What fur is this coat?

这件 外衣 是 什么 皮子 的?

Zhèjiàn wàiyī shì shénme pízi de?

Is this ···?

这是···?

Zhè shì ···?

beaver	eiderdown
水獭皮	鸭绒
shuǐtǎpí	**yāróng**
fox	fur inner lining
狐皮	皮筒
húpí	**pítǒng**
fur plates	imitation leather
皮板	人造革
píbǎn	**rénzàogé**
kidskin	lambskin
小山羊皮	小羊皮
xiǎoshānyángpí	**xiǎoyángpí**
leopard	lynx
豹皮	猞猁皮
bàopí	**shēlìpí**
mink	pony skin
白貂皮	马驹皮
báidiāopí	**mǎjūpí**

rabbit
家兔皮
jiātùpí

sable
黑貂皮
hēidiāopí

weasel
黄鼠狼皮
huángshǔlángpí

rabbit, wild
野兔皮
yětùpí

squirrel, grey
灰鼠皮
huīshǔpí

D. Shoes
鞋
xié

I need a pair of (black) (brown) ladies' leather shoes (sandals).

我　要　一双　（黑色）（咖啡色）女　皮鞋
Wǒ yào yìshuāng （hēisè）（kāfēisè）nǚ píxié
（凉鞋）。
（liángxié）。

These shoes are (a little tight) (too big).

鞋　(有点儿 紧)(太大)。

Xié (yǒudiǎnr jǐn) (tài dà).

Please show me a (larger) (smaller) size.

请 给　我(大一点儿)(小一点儿)　号码儿　的。

Qǐng gěi wǒ (dà yìdiǎnr)(xiǎo yìdiǎnr)hàomǎ de.

laces	overshoes
鞋带	套鞋
xiédàir	**tàoxié**
slippers	socks
拖鞋	袜子
tuōxié	**wàzi**
stockings	
女长袜	
nǚchángwà	

E. Stationery and Photographic Materials
文具和照像器材
Wénjù hé Zhàoxiàng Qìcái

ball-point pen
原珠笔
yuánzhūbǐ
Chinese brush
毛笔
máobǐ
Chinese ink stick
墨
mò
eraser
橡皮
xiàngpí
mucilage
胶水儿
jiāoshuǐr
paste
浆糊
jiànghú
water colours
水彩
shuǐcǎi
lens
镜头
jìngtóu

carbon paper
复写纸
fùxiězhǐ
Chinese ink box
墨盒儿
mòhér
envelope
信封
xìnfēng
fountain pen
自来水儿笔
zìláishuǐrbǐ
ink
墨水儿
mòshuǐr
notebook
笔记本儿
bǐjìběnr
ruler
尺子
chǐzi
writing paper
信纸
xìnzhǐ

tripod   photo album

三角架   影集

sānjiǎojià   **yǐngjí**

I'd like to see a camera.

我 想 看看 照像机。

Wǒ xiǎng kànkan zhàoxiàngjī.

What's the power of the lens of this camera?

这个 照像机 的 镜头 是 多大的？

Zhege zhàoxiàngjī de jìngtóu shì duō dà de?

I want some (135) (120) colour (black and white) film.

我 要 买 （一三五） （一二〇） 彩色 （黑白）

Wǒ yào mǎi(yāosānwǔ)(yāoèrlíng)cǎisè(hēibái)

胶卷儿。

jiāojuǎnr.

What is the speed of this film?

这个 胶卷儿 的 感光 速度 是 多少？

Zhège jiāojuǎnr de gǎnguāng sùdù shì duōshǎo?

F. Record Players, Records, Cassette Tape Recorders
留声机、唱片、盒式录音机
Liúshēngjī, Chàngpiàn, Héshì lùyīnjī

electronic music

电子　音乐

diànzǐyīnyuè

record of Chinese classical music

　中国　　　古典　音乐　唱片

Zhōngguó gǔdiǎn yīnyuè chàngpiàn

record of（Chinese folk songs）（dance music）
（opera）（symphony）

（中国　　民歌）（舞曲）（歌剧）（交响乐）

（Zhōngguó míngē）（wǔqǔ）（gējù）（jiāoxiǎngyuè）

唱片

chàngpiàn

stereo music

立体　音乐

lìtǐ　yīnyuè

cassette

盒式　磁带

héshì　cídài

G. Flowers and Birds
花、鸟
Huā , niǎo

Make me up （a bouquet）（a basket）of flowers，
please.

请　给我　选　（一束）（一篮子）花儿。

Qǐng gěi wǒ xuǎn （yíshù）（yìlánzi）huār.

What cut flowers have you?

你们　有　什么　鲜花儿　吗？

Nǐmen yǒu shénme xiānhuār ma?

We need a wreath of fresh flowers.

我们　要　一个　鲜花圈。

Wǒmen yào yíge xiānhuāquān.

Please put a ribbon on the wreath with the words
…

花圈　　上　要　一条　缎带，　　并且　写
Huāquān shàng yào yì tiáo duàndài，bìngqiě xiě

上　这些　字⋯
shang zhèxiē zì⋯

I'd like a (small) (large) potted plant.

我 要　一(小)　(大)　盆　花儿。
Wǒ yào yì (xiǎo) (dà) pén huār.

agave	asparagus fern
龙舌兰	文竹
lóngshélán	**wénzhú**
azalea	begonia
杜鹃花	秋海棠
dùjuānhuā	**qiūhǎitáng**
cactus	camellia
仙人掌	茶花
xiānrénzhǎng	**cháhuā**
canna	carnation
美人蕉	香石竹
měirénjiāo	**xiāngshízhú**
cassia	Chinese rose
桂花	月季
guìhuā	**yuèjì**

chrysanthemum	cock's comb
菊花	鸡冠花
júhuā	**jīguānhuā**
dahlia	daisy
西蕃莲	雏菊
xīfānlián	**chújú**
evergreen	fern
万年青	羊齿草
wànniánqīng	**yángchǐcǎo**
foxglove	gardenia
指顶花	白兰花
zhǐdǐnghuā	**báilánhuā**
geranium	gladiola
绣球花	菖兰
xiùqiúhuā	**chānglán**
hydrangea	hibiscus
紫绣球	芙蓉
zǐxiùqiú	**fúróng**
holly	honeysuckle
冬青	金银花
dōngqīng	**jīnyínhuā**
jasmine	lilac
茉莉	丁香
mòlì	**dīngxiāng**

lily
百合
bǎihé

lotus
荷花
héhuā

magnolia
木兰花
mùlánhuā

marigold
金盏花
jīnzhǎnhuā

morning glory
牵牛花
qiānniúhuā

narcissus
水仙
shuǐxiān

oleander
夹竹桃
jiāzhútáo

orchid
兰花
lánhuā

pansy
蝴蝶花
húdiéhuā

peony
芍药
sháoyào

pink
石竹
shízhú

poinsettia
一品红
yìpǐnhóng

poppy
婴粟花
yīngsùhuā

winter sweet
腊梅
làméi

rose
玫瑰
méiguī

snap-dragon
金鱼草
jīnyúcǎo

sweet pea	tuberose
豌豆花	玉簪花
wāndòuhuā	**yùzānhuā**
tulip	violet
郁金香	紫罗兰
yùjīnxiāng	**zǐluólán**
water lily	wood sorrel
水浮莲	酢浆草
shuǐfúlián	**zhàjiāngcǎo**
miniature garden	rockery
盆景	假山
pénjǐng	**jiǎshān**
canary	myna
金丝雀	八哥
jīnsīquè	**bāgē**
thrush	lark
画眉	百灵
huàméi	**bǎilíng**
parrot	oriole
鹦鹉	黄莺
yīngwǔ	**huángyīng**

H. Toys
玩具
Wánjù

What musical toys have you?

你们 有 什么 音乐 玩具 吗？

Nǐmen yǒu shénme yīnyuè wánjù ma?

Please show me some electronic toys.

请 给我拿 几个 电子 玩具 看看。

Qǐng gěi wǒ ná jǐge diànzǐ wánjù kànkan.

doll	building blocks	facemask
娃娃	积木	面具
wáwa	**jīmù**	**miànjù**

I. Daily Necessities
日用品
Rìyòngpǐn

belt	briefcase
皮带	皮包
pídài	**píbāo**
button	cap
纽扣	帽子
niǔkòu	**màozi**
cologne (Florida water)	cold cream
花露水	冷霜
huālùshuǐ	**lěngshuāng**
cosmetics	creme rinse
化妆品	染发液
huàzhuāngpǐn	**rǎnfàyè**
cuff link	eyebrow pencil
袖扣儿	描眉笔
xiùkòur	**miáoméibǐ**
face powder	fur hat
香粉	皮帽子
xiāngfěn	**pímàozi**
gloves	hair oil
手套儿	发油
shǒutàor	**fàyóu**

handkerchief	lipstick
手帕	口红
shǒupà	**kǒuhóng**
mirror	nail clippers
镜子	指甲刀
jìngzi	**zhǐjiǎdāo**
nail polish	necktie
指甲油	领带
zhǐjiǎyóu	**lǐngdài**
perfume	purse
香水	钱包
xiāngshuǐ	**qiánbāo**
razor (blade)	scarf
剃刀（刀片）	围巾
tìdāo(dāopiàn)	**wéijīn**
shoe polish	straw hat
鞋油	草帽
xiéyóu	**cǎomào**
talcum powder	toilet soap
爽身粉	香皂
shuǎngshēnfěn	**xiāngzào**
toilet paper	tooth brush
手纸	牙刷
shǒuzhǐ	**yáshuā**

tooth paste	towel
牙膏	毛巾
yágāo	**máojīn**
wallet	wig
皮夹子(钱夹儿)	假发
píjiāzi(qiánjiār)	**jiǎfà**

J. Books and Newspapers
书籍和报刊
Shūjí hé Bàokān

Where can I buy books in (Chinese) (English)?

哪儿 可以 买到 (中文) (英文) 书?

Nǎr kěyǐ mǎidào (Zhōngwén)(Yīngwén) shū?

I would like to see (Marxist-Leninist) (Chairman Mao's) works in English.

我 想 看 看 英文 的(马列) (毛

Wǒ xiǎng kànkan Yīngwén de (Mǎ-Liè)(Máo

主席) 著作。

Zhǔxí)zhùzuò.

I would like some Chinese literary works in English.

我 要 英文 的 中国 文学 书籍。

Wǒ yào Yīngwén de Zhōngguó wénxué shūjí.

I would like a （Chinese-English） （English-Chinese） dictionary.

我 要 一本 （汉英） （英汉） 字典。

Wǒ yào yìběn （Hàn-Yīng）（Yīng-Hàn）zìdiǎn.

I want to buy an English - Chinese pocket dictionary.

我 要 买 一本 袖珍 英汉 字典。

Wǒ yào mǎi yìběn xiùzhēn Yīng-Hàn zìdiǎn.

Do you have any tourist guide books on China in English?

你们 有 英文 的 中国 导游 书 吗？

Nǐmen yǒu Yīngwén de Zhōngguó dǎoyóu shū ma?

Please show me your latest （books） （periodicals）.

请 把 最新的 （书） （杂志）拿 给 我 看看。

Qǐng bǎ zuìxīn de（shū）（zázhì）ná gěi wǒ kànkan.

目录 在 哪儿？

Mùlù zài nǎr?

I should like to subscribe to some magazines. How shall I go about it?

我 想 订 几份 杂志，不 知道 怎么办

Wǒ xiǎng dìng jǐfèn zázhì，bù zhīdào zěnme bàn

手续？

shǒuxù？

Just fill in this form and pay here.

填 好 这 张 表，再 付钱 就 行 了。

Tián hǎo zhè zhāng biǎo，zài fùqián jiù xíng le.

Please show me some publications of the Academy of Sciences.

请 把 科学院的 刊物 拿 几本 给我

Qǐng bǎ kēxuéyuàn de kānwù ná jǐběn gěi wǒ

看看。

kànkan.

Has this book been translated into English?

这本 书 译成 英文 了吗？

Zhè běn shū yìchéng Yīngwén le ma？

Who is the translator?

译者 是 谁？

Yìzhě shì shuí？

Is this the commemorative edition?

这 是 纪念 版本 吗？

Zhè shì jìniàn bǎnběn ma？

Where can I get (children's) (agricultural) books?

在 哪儿 可以　买到　(儿童) (农业)　书籍？

Zài nǎr kěyǐ mǎidào (értóng)(nóngyè) shūjí?

author	circulation
作者	发行（发行量）
zuòzhě	**fāxíng（fāxíngliàng）**
cover	fable
封面	寓言
fēngmiàn	**yùyán**
fairy-tale	novel
童话	小说
tónghuà	**xiǎoshuō**
pamphlet	poet
小册子	诗人
xiǎocèzi	**shīrén**
short story	writer
短篇小说	作家
duǎnpiānxiǎoshuō	**zuòjiā**
editor	publisher
编辑	出版者
biānjí	**chūbǎnzhě**
publishing house	Foreign Languages Press
出版社	外文出版社
chūbǎnshè	**Wàiwén Chūbǎnshè**

frist volume

第一卷

dì-yī juàn

one-volume edition

一卷集

yī-juànjí

edition

版本

bǎnběn

second volume

第二卷

dì-èr juàn

two-volume edition

两卷集

liǎng-juàn jí

Please give me today's paper.

请 给 我 一 份 今天 的 报纸。

Qǐng gěi wǒ yífèn jintiān de bàozhǐ.

I want the lastest issue of (*Beijing Review*)(*China Today*)(*China Pictorial*), Please.

我 要 最新 一期 的 (《北京 周报》)

Wǒ yào zuì xīn yìqī de (《Běijīng Zhōubào》)

(《今日 中国》)(《人民画报》)。

(《Jīnrì Zhōngguó》)(《Rénmín Huàbào》).

How much is this (paper) (magazine)?

这 种 (报)(杂志) 多少 钱 一份儿?

Zhèzhǒng (bào)(zázhì) duōshǎo qián yífènr?

How often does this magazine come out?

这 种 杂志 多久 出 一期?

Zhèzhǒng zázhì duō jiǔ chū yì qī?

I want to subscribe to some newspapers and magazines in English.

我 要 订 英文 的 报纸 和 杂志。

Wǒ yào dìng Yīngwén de bàozhǐ hé zázhì.

Is it a (social-political) (literary) (popular-scientific) (sports) magazine?

这 是 (社会—政治) （文学） （科学普及）

Zhè shì (shèhuì-zhèngzhì)(wénxué)(kēxué pǔjí)

（体育） 杂志 吗？

(tǐyù) zázhì ma?

What literary magazines do you publish?

你们 出 些 什么 文学 杂志？

Nǐmen chū xiē shénme wénxué zázhì?

daily	People's Daily
日报	《人民日报》
rìbào	《**Rénmín Rìbào**》
editor, editor-in-chief	editorial board
编辑、总编辑	编辑部
biānjí、zǒngbiānjí	**biānjíbù**
journalist	local paper
新闻工作者	地方报纸
xīnwén gōngzuòzhě	**dìfāng bàozhǐ**

news agency	reporter
通讯社	记者
tōngxùnshè	**jìzhě**
special correspondent	news photographer
特派记者	摄影记者
tèpài jìzhě	**shèyǐng jìzhě**
quarterly	weekly
季刊	周刊
jìkān	**zhōukān**
monthly	fortnightly
月刊	半月刊
yuèkān	**bànyuèkān**
advertisement	
广告	
guǎnggào	

K. Miscellaneous

其它

Qítā

Please give me a set of postcards with (grottoes)

(the West Lake) views.

请 给 我 一套（石窟）（西湖） 景色的

Qǐng gěi wǒ yítào (shíkū) (Xī Hú) jǐngsè de

明信片。

míngxìnpiàn.

I have broken my glasses, can you repair them?

我 的 眼镜 坏了， 能 修理 一下 吗？

Wǒ de yǎnjìng huàile, néng xiūlǐ yíxià ma?

Can I change foreign currency in the shop?

商店 里 可以 换 货币 吗？

Shāngdiàn lǐ kěyǐ huàn huòbì ma?

I want to buy some gifts for my friends at home.

我 想 给 家里的 朋友 买 几件 礼物。

Wǒ xiǎng gěi jiālǐ de péngyǒu mǎi jǐjiàn lǐwù.

Can I take this out of the country?

我 可以把 这个 带到 外国 去吗？

Wǒ kěyǐ bǎ zhège dàidào wàiguó qù ma?

Wrap them up all together, please.

请 把 所有 的 东西 包在 一起。

Qǐng bǎ suǒyǒu de dōngxi bāo zài yìqǐ.

Please give me a receipt.

请 开 发票。

Qǐng kāi fāpiào.

7. CULTURAL AND SPORTS ACTIVITIES

文化和体育活动

Wénhuà hé Tǐyù Huódòng

A. At a Theatre

剧院

Jùyuàn

I'd like to see a play.

我 想 看 戏。

Wǒ xiǎng kàn xì.

What's on at the theatre today?

今天 剧院 演 什么?

Jīntiān jùyuàn yǎn shénme?

Is it a play by a well-known writer?

是 名 作家 写的 剧本 吗?

Shì míng zuòjiā xiěde jùběn ma?

I'm very interested in (modern drama) (tragedy)
(comedy) (Beijing opera) (local opera) (opera).

我 对 （话剧）（悲剧）（喜剧）（京剧）（地方戏）

Wǒ duì(huàjù)(bēijù)(xǐjù)(jīngjù)(dìfāngxì)

（歌剧） 很 感 兴趣。

(gējù)hěn gǎn xìngqù.

How much is a ticket in the front rows?

前 几 排 的 票 多少 钱 一张？

Qián jǐ pái de piào duōshǎo qián yìzhāng?

Where do I get a programme?

哪儿 卖 节目单？

Nǎr mài jiémùdān?

Our seats are too (far away) (near).

我们 的 座位 太（远）（近）了。

Wǒmen de zuòwèi tài(yuǎn) (jìn) le.

Who wrote it?

剧 作者 是 谁？

Jù zuòzhě shì shuí?

Who plays the main role?

谁 演 主角儿？

Shuí yǎn zhǔjuér?

What troupe is performing today?

今天　是　哪个　团　演出？
Jīntiān shì něige tuán yǎnchū?

actor	actress
男演员	女演员
nányǎnyuán	**nǔyǎnyuán**
art director	chorus conductor
艺术指导	合唱指挥
yìshù zhǐdǎo	**héchàng zhǐhuī**
opera singer	puppet theatre
歌剧演员	木偶剧院
gējù yǎnyuán	**mùǒu jùyuàn**
solo	song and dance
独唱	歌舞
dúchàng	**gēwǔ**
musical accompaniment	scenery
伴奏	布景
bànzòu	**bùjǐng**

B. At a Cinema

电影院

Diànyǐngyuàn

What's on at the cinema today?

今天 演 什么 电影？

Jīntiān yǎn shénme diànyǐng?

We want to see the latest feature film.

我 们 想 看 新 出 的 故事 片。

Wǒmen xiǎng kàn xīn chūde gùshi piān.

When do the （evening）（matinée） performances begin?

（晚）（日） 场 什么 时候 开始？

(Wǎn)(Rì)chǎng shénme shíhou kāishǐ?

Who directed this film?

这个 影片 的 导演 是 谁？

Zhège yǐngpiàn de dǎoyǎn shì shuí?

Who wrote the script?

电影 剧本 的 作者 是谁？

Diànyǐng jùběn de zuòzhě shì shuí?

Who composed the music?

谁　作的　　曲子?

Shuí zuò de qǔzi?

In which year did this film first appear?

这部　影片　　是　哪年　　上映 的?

Zhèbù yǐngpiàn shì něinián shàngyìng de?

In which studio was the film made?

这部　影片　　是　哪个　制片厂　　拍的?

Zhèbù yǐngpiàn shì něige zhìpiànchǎng pāidè?

Is it a foreign film?

是　外国　　影片　吗?

Shì wàiguó yǐngpiàn ma?

I'm interested in (feature films) (popular scientific films) (cartoons) (documentary films) (news reels).

我　喜欢　看(　故事片)　(科教片)　(动画

Wǒ xǐhuān kàn(gùshì piān)(kējiào piān)(dònghuà

片)　(纪录片)　(新闻片)。

piān)(jìlùpiān)(xīnwén piān).

cinema

电影院

diànyǐngyuàn

film actor

电影演员

diànyǐng yǎnyuán

105

film festival	film studio
电影节	电影制片厂
diànyǐngjié	**diànyǐng zhìpiànchǎng**
hero in the film	photographer
影片主角	摄影师
yǐngpiàn zhǔjué	**shèyǐngshī**
screen	wide-screen film
银幕	宽银幕影片
yínmù	**kuānyínmù yǐngpiàn**

C. At a Concert
音乐会
Yīnyuèhuì

I like (folk) (classical) (symphonic) music.

我　喜欢　（民间）　（古典）　（交响）　音乐。

Wǒ xǐhuān (mínjiān)(gǔdiǎn)(jiāoxiǎng) yīnyuè.

Where is the concert?

音乐会　在　哪儿　举行？

Yīnyuèhuì zài nǎr jǔxíng?

106

What's today's programme?

今天　有　哪些　节目？

Jīntiān yǒu něixiē jiémù?

Can I take a recorder? May I record it?

我　可以　带录音机　吗？我　可以　录音　吗？

Wǒ kěyǐ dài lùyīnjī ma? Wǒ kěyǐ lùyìn ma?

Where can I obtain a recording of that music?

在 哪儿 可以 买到　这个　乐曲　的　唱片？

Zài nǎr kěyǐ mǎidào zhège yuèqǔ de chàngpiàn?

Do you often go to concerts?

您　常　去　参加　音乐会　吗？

Nín cháng qù cānjiā yīnyuèhuì ma?

What instruments do you like to play?

您　喜欢　演奏　哪种　乐器？

Nín xǐhuān yǎnzòu něizhǒng yuèqì?

I'd like to buy one of those two-stringed fiddles.

我　想买　一个　二胡。

Wǒ xiǎng mǎi yíge èrhú.

accordion	cello
手风琴	大提琴
shǒufēngqín	**dàtíqín**
clarinet	flute
黑管	长笛
hēiguǎn	**chángdí**

guitar	harp
吉他	竖琴
jítā	**shùqín**
oboe	piano
双簧管	钢琴
shuānghuángguǎn	**gāngqín**
trumpet	Chinese musical instrument
小号	民族乐器
xiǎohào	**mínzú yuèqì**

Who is the vocal soloist?

独唱 演员 是 谁？

Dúchàng yǎnyuán shì shuí？

Who's the (conductor) (accompanist)?

（指挥） （伴奏） 是 谁？

（Zhǐhuī）（Bànzòu）shì shuí？

What do you think of the concert?

您 觉得 音乐会 怎么样？

Nín juéde yīnyuèhuì zěnmeyàng？

baritone	bass
男中音	男低音
nánzhōngyīn	**nándīyīn**
alto	mezzo-soprano
女低音	女中音
nǚdīyīn	**nǚzhōngyīn**

duet

二重唱

èrchóngchàng

overture

序曲

xùqǔ

quartet

四重奏

sìchóngzòu (instrumental)

trio

三重奏

sānchóngzòu (instrumental)

quintet

五重奏

wǔchóngzòu (instrumental)

soprano

女高音

nǚgāoyīn

dance music

舞曲

wǔqǔ

四重唱

sìchóngchàng (vocal)

三重唱

sānchóngchàng (vocal)

五重唱

wǔchóngchàng (vocal)

tenor

男高音

nángāoyīn

D. Sports
体育
Tǐyù

I like seeing football games very much.

我 很 喜欢 看 足球 比赛。

Wǒ hěn xǐhuān kàn zúqiú bǐsài.

badminton	basketball
羽毛球	篮球
yǔmáoqiú	**lánqiú**
table tennis	tennis
乒乓球	网球
pīngpāngqiú	**wǎngqiú**
volleyball	water polo
排球	水球
páiqiú	**shuǐqiú**

Where will the gymnastic show be?

体操 表演 在 哪儿 举行?

Tǐcāo biǎoyǎn zài nǎr jǔxíng?

What's the capacity of the (Capital Gymnasium)

(Workers' Gymnasium)(Workers' Stadium)?

(首都　　体育馆)　　(工人　　体育馆)　(工人

(Shǒudū Tǐyùguǎn)(Gōngrén Tǐyùguǎn)(Gōngrén

体育场)　　有　多少　座位?

Tǐyùchǎng) yǒu duōshǎo zuòwèi?

When was it built?

哪年　建成　的?

Něinián jiànchéng de?

What sport do you like best?

您　最　喜欢　哪项　体育　活动?

Nín zuì xǐhuān něixiàng tǐyù huódòng?

Do you often go (swimming)(skiing)(skating)
(mountaineering)?

您　经常　　(游泳)　(滑雪)　(滑冰)

Nín jīngcháng (yóuyǒng)(huáxuě)(huábīng)

(爬山)　吗?

(páshān)ma?

Is there a swimming pool near here?

附近　有　游泳　池　吗?

Fùjìn yǒu yóuyǒng chí ma?

We'd like to go and see track and field events.

我们　想　看　田径　比赛。

Wǒmen xiǎng kàn tiánjìng bǐsài.

Is this a semi-final or a final match?

这场　　是　半决赛，还是　决赛？

Zhècháng shì bànjuésài, hái shì juésài?

We've come to take part in the (invitational tournament) (friendship match) (championships).

我们　是　来　参加(邀请赛)　(友谊赛)

Wǒmen shì lái cānjiā(yāoqǐngsài)(yǒuyìsài)

(锦标赛)的。

(jǐnbiāosài) de.

captain	coach
队长	教练员
duìzhǎng	**jiàoliànyuán**
goal keeper	referee
守门员	裁判员
shǒuményuán	**cáipànyuán**
score keeper	spectators
计分员	观众
jìfēnyuán	**guānzhòng**
sportsman	
运动员	
yùndòngyuán	

E. Acrobatics and Circus
杂技和马戏
Zájì hé Mǎxì

I've been looking forward to a Chinese (acrobatic) (circus) show for ages.

我 一直 在 盼望 着 看 一场 中国

Wǒ yìzhí zài pànwàngzhe kàn yìcháng Zhōngguó

（杂技）（马戏） 表演。

（zájì）（mǎxì）biǎoyǎn.

Where will the show be given?

杂技 在 哪儿 演出？

Zájì zài nǎr yǎnchū?

Which acrobatic troupe is performing tonight?

今晚 哪个 杂技团 演出？

Jīnwǎn něige zájì tuán yǎnchū?

How old are these young acrobats, and how long have they been trained?

这些 青年 演员 有 多大？ 他们

Zhèxiē qīngnián yǎnyuán yǒu duōdà?Tāmen

训练 多长 时间 了？

xùnliàn duōcháng shíjiān le?

The show was fantastic! Especially the lion dance and the trapeze were really great!

这 场 演出 太好 了！特别 是 狮子舞 和

Zhècháng yǎnchū tàihǎole! Tèbié shì shīziwǔ hé

空中 飞人， 真 了不起！

kōngzhōng fēirén, zhēn liǎobùqǐ!

It was a really great show. I'd like to see it again.

演出 真 有 意思。我 还想 再看 一遍。

Yǎnchū zhēn yǒu yìsi. Wǒ háixiǎng zài kàn yíbiàn.

It has been a wonderful evening. I've really enjoyed it.

今晚 过得 真有 意思。 我 非常 愉快。

Jīnwǎn guòde zhēn yǒu yìsi. Wǒ fēicháng yúkuài.

I think the martial art performed by the children was really super.

我 觉得 那几个 小孩儿 表演 的 武术

Wǒ juéde nèi jǐ ge xiǎohái biǎoyǎn de wǔshù

真好。

zhēnhǎo.

8. SEEING A DOTOR

看病

Kànbìng

I don't feel well.

我 不大 舒服。

Wǒ bú dà shūfu.

I'm afraid I have a cold.

恐 怕 我 感冒了。

Kǒngpà wǒ gǎnmào le.

I have a (headache) (stomach-ache) (tooth-ache) (sore throat)(ear-ache).

我 （头）（胃）（牙）（喉咙） （耳朵） 疼。

Wǒ tóu (wèi) (yá) (hóulóng) (ěrduo) téng.

I have something in my eye.

我 眼睛 里 进去了 东西。

Wǒ yǎnjing lǐ jìnqùle dōngxi.

I have a (cough) (diarrhoea) (vomiting)(constipation).

我（咳嗽）（泄肚）（呕吐）（便秘）。

Wǒ（késou）（xièdù）（ǒutù）（biànmì）.

I've rubbed a blister on my heel.

我　脚上　打了个泡。

Wǒ jiǎoshang dǎle ge pào.

I want to see a physician.

我　要　看　内科　医生。

Wǒ yào kàn nèikē yīshēng.

dentist	E. N. T. specialist
牙科医生	耳鼻喉科医生
yákē yīshēng	**ěrbíhóukē yīshēng**
gynaecologist	oculist
妇科医生	眼科医生
fùkē yīshēng	**yǎnkē yīshēng**
paediatrician	surgeon
儿科医生	外科医生
érkē yīshēng	**wàikē yīshēng**

Would you please call a doctor for me?

请　给　我　请　个　医生　来　好　吗？

Qǐng gěi wǒ qǐng ge yīshēng lái hǎo ma？

It (hurts) (is uncomfortable) here.

我　这里　（疼）　（不舒服）。

Wǒ zhèli（téng）（bù shūfu）.

116

I have a pain here.

这里 疼。

Zhèlǐ téng.

I feel feverish (I have a chill).

我 发烧 （我 发冷）。

Wǒ fāshāo (Wǒ fālěng).

I'd like to have my blood pressure tested.

我 想 量 一下 血压。

Wǒ xiǎng liáng yíxià xuèyā.

I have had (malaria) (pneumonia) (tuberculosis) (dysentery).

我 得过 （疟疾）（肺炎）（肺结核）（痢疾）。

Wǒ déguo (nüèji) (fèiyán) (fèijiéhé) (lìji).

I have had (measles) (scarlet fever) (typhus).

我 得过 （麻疹） （猩红热） （斑疹

Wǒ déguo (mázhěn) (xīnghóngrè) (bānzhěn

伤寒）。

shānghán).

I began to feel ill (yesterday) (the day before yesterday).

我 （昨天） （前天） 开始 感觉 不 舒服。

Wǒ (zuótiān) (qiántiān) kāishǐ gǎnjué bù shūfu.

How shall I take the medicine?

药　怎么　吃？

Yào zěnme chī?

I feel (better) (worse) (the same).

我　感觉　（好些）　（更　不舒服）　（一个　样）。

Wǒ gǎnjué (hǎo xiē) (gèng bù shūfu) (yíge yàng).

The medicine was (good) (no use).

这　药　（效果　不错）　（不起　作用）。

Zhè yào (xiàoguǒ búcuò) (bùqǐ zuòyòng).

Does my condition require surgery?

我　的病　需要　做　手术　吗？

Wǒ de bìng xūyào zuò shǒushù ma?

Can you (fill) (extract) a tooth for me?

您　能　给　我（补）　（拔）个　牙吗？

Nín néng gěi wǒ (bǔ) (bá) ge yá ma?

I've sprained my ankle.

我　脚腕子　扭伤　了。

Wǒ jiǎowànzi niǔshāngle.

acute (chronic) disease

急性　（慢性）　病

jíxìng (mànxìng) bìng

acupuncture anaesthesia　　　bandage

针灸麻醉　　　　　　　　　　绷带

zhēnjiǔ mázuì　　　　　　**bēngdài**

118

burn

烧伤

shāoshāng

general anaesthesia

全身麻醉

quánshēn mázuì

infectious (contagious)
disease

传染病

chuánrǎn bìng

inflammation

发炎

fāyán

fracture

骨折

gǔzhé

infection

传染

chuánrǎn

injection

打针

dǎzhēn

local anaesthesia

局部麻醉

júbù mázuì

(Five drops) (one graduation on the bottle) (one tablet) (one spoon) to be taken three times a day.

一天 三次， 每次（五滴）（一格）（一片）（一勺）。

Yìtiān sāncì，měicì（wǔdī）（yìgé）（yípiàn）（yìsháo）.

9. EVERYDAY WORDS AND EXPRESSIONS

常用词和常用语

Chángyòng Cí hé Chángyòng Yǔ

I	you (sing.), you (pl.)
我	你，您， 你们， 您们
wǒ	**nǐ nín nǐmén nínmen**
he	she
他	她
tā	**tā**
we	they
我们	他们
wǒmen	**tāmen**
yes	no
是(对)	不(不是),(不对)
shì（duì）	**bù（búshì）,（búduì）**
please	perhaps
请	可能
qǐng	**kěnéng**

120

I don't understand.

我　不　懂。

Wǒ bù dǒng.

Thank you. Thank you very much.

谢谢。 非常　　感谢。

Xièxie. Fēicháng gǎnxiè.

Sorry, I'm so sorry.

对 不 起。真　对 不 起。

Duìbùqǐ, zhēn duìbùqǐ.

Good.

好。

Hǎo.

It's allowed.

可以。

Kěyǐ.

It's not allowed.

不　可以。

Bù kěyǐ.

I like it.

我喜欢。

Wǒ xǐhuān.

I don't like it.

我　不喜欢。

Wǒ bù xǐhuān.

I want it.

我 想 要。

Wǒ xiǎngyào.

I don't want it.

我 不 想要。

Wǒ bù xiǎngyào.

I've forgotten.

我 忘了。

Wǒ wàngle.

Please don't forget it.

请 别 忘了。

Qǐng bié wàngle.

I'm tired.

我 累了。

Wǒ lèile.

I need a rest.

我 需要 休息 一下。

Wǒ xūyào xiūxi yíxià.

It's necessary.

有必要。

Yǒu bìyào.

It's not necessary.

没有 必要。

122

Méiyǒu bìyào

(much) (many), too (much) (many)

(多) ，(太多)

(duō)，(tàiduō)

(little) (few), too (little) (few)

(少) ，(太少)

(shǎo)，(tàishǎo)

cheap	enough
贱 （便宜）	够了
jiàn (piányi)	**gòule**
all	where
全部	哪里
quánbù	**nǎlǐ**
there	here
那里	这里
nàlǐ	**zhèlǐ**
far	near
远	近
yuǎn	**jìn**
inside	outside
里边	外边
lǐbiān	**wàibiān**

upstairs	downstairs
楼上	楼下
lóushàng	**lóuxià**
forward	backward
向前	向后
xiàngqián	**xiànghòu**
to the right	to the left
向右	向左
xiàngyòu	**xiàngzuǒ**
on the right	on the left
在右边	在左边
zài yòubiān	**zài zuǒbiān**
on the other side (over there)	at once, now
在那边	马上,现在
zài nàbiān	**mǎshàng,xiànzài**
soon (quick)	spring
快	春天
kuài	**chūntiān**
summer	autumn
夏天	秋天
xiàtiān	**qiūtiān**

winter

冬天

dōngtiān

I'm hot.

我觉得热。

Wǒ juéde rè.

I can't hear.

我听不见。

Wǒ tīng bú jiàn.

because

因为

yīnwèi

farewell

以后再见

yǐhòu zàijiàn

I'm cold.

我觉得冷。

wǒ juéde lěng.

I can't see.

我看不见。

Wǒ kàn bú jiàn.

Why?

为什么?

Wèi shénme?

goodbye

再见

zàijiàn

see you again

再见

zàijiàn

Please (accept) (take) this.

请 您 (接受) (拿) 这个。

Qǐng nín (jiēshòu) (ná) zhège.

Please sit down.

请 坐。

Qǐng zuò.

Please show me …

请 把 … 拿 给 我 看看。

125

Qǐng bǎ ··· ná gěi wǒ kànkan.

Please pass me····.

请把 ··· 递 给 我。

Qǐng bǎ... dì gěi wǒ.

Please help.

请 您 帮 帮 忙。

Qǐng nín bāngbāng máng.

It's (beautiful) (interesting)!

真 （漂亮） （有意思）!

Zhēn (piàoliang) (yǒu yìsi)!

What's it called?

这 叫 什么?

Zhè jiào shénme?

How much does it cost?

这 要 多少 钱?

Zhè yào duōshǎo qián?

five yuan

五块

wǔkuài

three yuan and fifty-two fen

三块五毛二

sānkuài wǔmáoèr

no charge

免费

miǎnfèi

What does this word mean?

这个 字 是　什么　意思？

Zhège zì shì shénme yìsi?

What did (he) (you) say?

（他）　（您）　说　什么？

(Tā)（Nín）shuō shénme?

Who will accompany us?

谁　陪　我们？

Shuí péi wǒmen?

Will you come with us?

您　和　我们　一起　去吗？

Nín hé wǒmen yìqǐ qù ma?

At what time must we be ready?

我们　必须　在 几点　准备　好？

Wǒmen bìxū zài jǐdiǎn zhǔnbèi hǎo?

Where do we meet?

在　哪儿　见面？

Zài nǎr jiànmiàn?

When shall we be back?

我们　什么　时候　回来？

Wǒmen shénme shíhou huílái?

Have we got time?

我们 有 时间 吗?

Wǒmen yǒu shíjiān ma?

How long will it take?

这 需要 多少 时间?

Zhè xūyào duōshǎo shíjiān?

When shall we start?

我们 什么 时候 动身?

Wǒmen shénme shíhou dòngshēn?

Is there any change in schedule?

时间 安排 有 什么 变化 吗?

Shíjiān ānpái yǒu shénme biànhuà ma?

There's a cancellation. We're not making the special excursion trip to the (West) (East) Tombs.

取消 了 一项 节目。我们 不 专门 去

Qǔxiāo le yíxiàng jiémù. Wǒmen bù zhuānmén qù

(西陵) (东陵) 了。

(Xīlíng) (Dōnglíng) le.

What's written here?

这里 写 的 是 什么?

Zhèlǐ xiěde shì shénme?

citizen	democracy
公民	民主
gōngmín	**mínzhǔ**

friendship

友谊

yǒuyì

peace

和平

hépíng

baggage claim tag

行李 标签

xíngli biāoqiān

boarding card

登机牌

dēngjīpái

cabin luggage

手提 行李

shǒutí xíngli

check in (at an airport)

办 乘机 手续

bàn chéngjī shǒuxù

check in (at a hotel)

办 住宿 手续

bàn zhùsù shǒuxù

check out (from a hotel)

办 结帐 手续

bàn jiézhàng shǒuxù

connecting flight

连续 飞行

liánxù fēixíng

exchange rate

兑换 率

duìhuàn lù

economy class

普通 座位

pǔtōng zuòwèi

foreign exchange

外汇

wàihuì

ongoing reservation	open-dated return
联运　订座	不定期　　往返　票
liányùn dìngzuò	**bùdìngqī wǎngfǎn piào**
passport	passport control
护照	护照　检查　站
hùzhào	**hùzhào jiǎnchá zhàn**
pedestrian crossing	quarantine
人行　横道	卫生　　站
rénxíng héngdào	**wèishēng zhàn**
subway	China Art Gallery
地下　铁道　（地铁）	中国　　美术馆
dìxià tiědào(dìtiě)	**Zhōngguó Měishùguǎn**
vaccination certifi-cate	Tian'anmen Square
注射　　证明	天安门　　广场
zhùshè zhèngmíng	**Tiān'ānmén Guǎngchǎng**
Great Hall of the People	Museum of Chinese History
人民　　大　会堂	中国　　历史
Rénmín Dà Huìtáng	**Zhōngguó Lìshǐ**
Monument to the People's Heroes	博物馆
	Bówùguǎn

人民　　英雄
Rénmín Yīngxióng
纪念碑
Jìniànbēi

attention
注意
zhùyì

exit
出口　　（太平门）
chūkǒu (tàipíngmén)

booking office
售票处
shòupiàochù

traveller's cheque
旅行　　支票
lǚxíng zhīpiào

full-fare ticket
全价票
quánjiàpiào

quarter-fare ticket
四分之一　价票
sìfēnzhīyī jià piào

Museum of the
Chinese Revolution
中国　　革命
Zhōngguó Gémìng
博物馆
Bówùguǎn

entrance
入口
rùkǒu

lift (elevator)
电梯
diàntī

information desk
问讯　台
wènxùntái

half-fare ticket
半价票
bànjià piào

no smoking
禁止　吸烟
jìnzhǐ xīyān

smoking room

吸烟 室

xīyānshì

lounge

休息室

xiūxishì

ladies' room

女厕所

nǔ cèsuǒ

men's room

男厕所

nán cèsuǒ

no exit

禁止 通行

jìnzhǐ tōngxíng

telephone

电话

diànhuà

Have a pleasant journey!

一路 顺风! (旅行 愉快!)

Yílù shùnfēng!（Lǔxíng yúkuài!）

Happy New Year!(Merry Christmas!)

新年 快乐! (圣诞节 快乐)!

Xīnnián kuàilè!（Shèngdànjié kuàilè!）

Many happy returns of the day!

祝 您 长寿!

Zhù nín chángshòu!

Sunday

星期天

Xīngqītiān

Monday

星期一

Xīngqīyī

Tuesday

星期二

Xīngqièr

Wednesday

星期三

Xīngqīsān

Thursday	Friday
星期四	星期五
Xīngqīsì	**Xīngqīwǔ**
Saturday	weekend
星期六	周末
Xīngqīliù	**zhōumò**
day	week
日	星期
rì	**xīngqī**
month	year
月	年
yuè	**nián**
January	February
一月	二月
Yīyuè	**Èryuè**
March	April
三月	四月
Sānyuè	**Sìyuè**
May	June
五月	六月
Wǔyuè	**Liùyuè**
July	August
七月	八月
Qīyuè	**Bāyuè**

September	October
九月	十月
Jiǔyuè	**Shíyuè**
November	December
十一月	十二月
Shíyīyuè	**Shíèryuè**
one	two
一	二
yī	**èr**
three	four
三	四
sān	**sì**
five	six
五	六
wǔ	**liù**
seven	eight
七	八
qī	**bā**
nine	ten
九	十
jiǔ	**shí**
eleven	twelve
十一	十二
shíyī	**shíèr**

thirteen	fourteen
十三	十四
shísān	**shísì**
fifteen	sixteen
十五	十六
shíwǔ	**shíliù**
seventeen	eighteen
十七	十八
shíqī	**shíbā**
nineteen	twenty
十九	二十
shíjiǔ	**èrshí**
thirty	forty
三十	四十
sānshí	**sìshí**
fifty	sixty
五十	六十
wǔshí	**liùshí**
seventy	eighty
七十	八十
qīshí	**bāshí**
ninety	one hundred
九十	一百
jiǔshí	**yībǎi**

two hundred

二百

èrbǎi

four hundred

四百

sìbǎi

six hundred

六百

liùbǎi

eight hundred

八百

bābǎi

one thousand

一千

yīqiān

one hundred thousand

十万

shíwàn

one hundred million

一亿

yīyì

three hundred

三百

sānbǎi

five hundred

五百

wǔbǎi

seven hundred

七百

qībǎi

nine hundred

九百

jiǔbǎi

ten thousand

一万

yīwàn

a million

一百万

yībǎiwàn

which? (ordinal number)	first
第几？	第一
dìjǐ?	**dìyī**
second	third
第二	第三
dìèr	**dìsān**
fourth	fifth
第四	第五
dìsì	**dìwǔ**
sixth	seventh
第六	第七
dìliù	**dìqī**
eighth	ninth
第八	第九
dìbā	**dìjiǔ**
tenth	1/2
第十	二分之一（一半）
dìshí	**èrfēn zhīyī（yíbàn）**
2/3	3/4
三分之二	四分之三
sānfēn zhièr	**sìfēn zhīsān**

4/5
五分之四
wǔfēn zhīsì

1.23
一点二三
yīdiǎn èrsān

half a dozen
半打
bàndá

ten pieces
十个(十件)十条
shíge shíjiàn shítiáo

one half
半个
bànge

G.M.T.
格林威治时间
Gélínwēizhì shíjiān

20:20
二十点二十
èrshídiǎn èrshí

0.5
零点五
língdiǎn wǔ

a pair
一双(一对,一付)
yìshuāng(yíduì,yífù)

one dozen
一打
yìdá

a hundred pieces
一百个
yìbǎige

local time
当地时间
dāngdì shíjiān

08:20
八点二十
bādiǎn èrshí

International Date Line
国际日期线
Guójì Rìqī Xiàn

00:00

零点

língdiǎn

6:00 a.m.

早晨　（上午）六点

zǎochén（shàngwǔ）liùdiǎn

6:00 p.m.

下午　（晚上）六点

xiàwǔ（wǎnshang）liùdiǎn

责任编辑：龙燕俐
装帧设计：朱　丹

学中国话手册

程　荒

＊

©华语教学出版社
华语教学出版社出版
（中国北京百万庄路 24 号）
邮政编码 100037
电　话：86-010-68326333
　　　　86-010-68994599
传　真：86-010-68326642
电子信箱：sinolingua@ihw.com.cn
北京外文印刷厂印刷
中国国际图书贸易总公司发行
（中国北京车公庄西路 35 号）
北京邮政信箱第 399 号　邮政编码 100044
1981 年（40 开）第一版
1996 年第二版
1999 年第二次印刷
（英）
ISBN 7-80052-048-X / H · 192(外)
定价：8.00 元
9－E－1513P